UNLOCKING WEALTH
45 AI STRATEGIES TO FINANCIAL FREEDOM

By Kyle Rae

Contents

PREFACE

"Unlocking Wealth: 45 AI Strategies to Financial Freedom" is an insightful guide that delves into the transformative power of artificial intelligence (AI) in the financial world. This comprehensive eBook demystifies the intricate world of AI and its implications for wealth creation, providing a roadmap for anyone—whether a seasoned investor, entrepreneur, or a novice looking to improve their financial situation.

This book will take you on a journey through the fascinating world of AI, starting with its impact on the global economy and businesses, and its potential for wealth generation. You'll understand the basics of AI and how to identify opportunities in various industries. You'll also discover how to cultivate an AI-focused mindset—essential for navigating the AI-centric financial landscape of the future.

Specific sections of the book explore how AI tools and strategies can optimize personal finance management, from AI-driven investment platforms and robo-advisors to automated savings and budgeting tools. For those interested in stock trading, you'll learn how AI is revolutionizing the stock market through algorithmic trading and AI-powered stock analysis. The book also covers how AI is transforming the real estate sector, providing smart property management solutions and real estate investment analysis tools.

If you're an entrepreneur or involved in e-commerce, you'll find invaluable insights into AI-powered product recommendation engines, inventory management, personalized marketing, and much more. There are even chapters dedicated to emerging trends like AI as a Service (AIaaS), AI in content creation, and AI for intellectual property and licensing.

In the final sections, the book discusses how AI can fuel startup and entrepreneurial endeavors, offering strategies for AI-driven market research, building and scaling AI-powered startups, and securing funding for AI-focused ventures.

"Unlocking Wealth: 45 AI Strategies to Financial Freedom" wraps up with a forward-looking conclusion, embracing the AI revolution for financial growth, predicting future prospects in AI, and offering actionable steps to implement the strategies discussed for financial freedom.

This eBook is not just a manual—it's a visionary guide for anyone looking to harness the power of AI for wealth creation. Whether you are a seasoned professional or an aspiring entrepreneur, this book will equip you with the knowledge and tools to navigate the AI revolution and unlock new avenues for financial growth.

Introduction

Welcome to "Unlocking Wealth: 45 AI Strategies to Financial Freedom." In an era where technological advancements are reshaping every facet of our lives, artificial intelligence (AI) emerges as one of the most transformative forces. From personal assistance to business operations, AI has found its place in virtually every sector. Its impact is particularly profound in the sphere of finance and wealth creation. This book aims to guide you on a journey to harness this powerful technology for your financial success.

AI's influence is not confined to sci-fi movies or tech giants' labs. It is a reality that has permeated our world, altering the way we live, work, and even think about the future. According to PwC, AI could add up to $15.7 trillion to the global economy by 2030. This tremendous potential for economic growth presents a unique opportunity for individuals and businesses alike to significantly boost their wealth.

However, the key to tapping into this potential lies in understanding AI and its applications. Without knowledge of its capabilities and how to utilize it, AI is just a buzzword. This book aims to simplify AI, breaking it down into digestible insights and actionable strategies that can lead you to financial freedom.

Over the course of this book, we will explore 45 unique strategies that center around leveraging AI for wealth creation. These strategies will span various sectors, from personal finance and the stock market to real estate and e-commerce, as well as innovative areas such as AI as a Service (AIaaS), content creation, intellectual property, and startups.

This book is designed for everyone from complete beginners with a curiosity about AI to seasoned professionals looking to expand their knowledge and drive their financial growth. By the end of this journey, you will have a robust understanding of how to use AI to your advantage in the financial world. You will be equipped with practical strategies and tips to capitalize on AI's potential and unlock your path to financial freedom.

The future of wealth creation is here. It's smart, it's transformative, and it's powered by AI. Are you ready to unlock your wealth with AI? Let's get started.

The Impact of AI on the Global Economy

Artificial intelligence (AI) is fundamentally transforming the global economy, with the potential to substantially boost economic growth, productivity, and job creation. As AI applications continue to expand across various industries, the technology is driving new business models, improving efficiency, and enabling cost savings. According to a study by PwC, AI has the potential to contribute up to $15.7 trillion to the global economy by 2030, with roughly $6.6 trillion coming from increased productivity and $9.1 trillion from consumption side-effects.

AI is disrupting traditional industries, making businesses rethink their strategies and adapt to a rapidly changing environment. Machine learning, natural language processing, computer vision, and other AI technologies are enabling the automation of a wide range of tasks, previously carried out by humans. This automation not only increases efficiency but also frees up human resources to focus on more strategic and creative aspects of work. As a result, AI is expected to lead to a significant shift in the global workforce, with a demand for skilled professionals who can work with and alongside AI technologies.

The Impact of AI on Businesses

The integration of AI into businesses across sectors has created new opportunities for innovation and growth. From streamlining operations and enhancing decision-making processes to personalizing customer experiences and optimizing supply chains, AI is revolutionizing the way companies operate.

In manufacturing, AI-driven automation is enabling companies to produce goods more efficiently, reduce waste, and cut costs. Smart factories that leverage AI technologies, such as machine learning and computer vision, can detect defects in products and streamline assembly lines, leading to increased productivity and improved quality control.

In the healthcare sector, AI is playing a critical role in drug discovery, diagnostics, and personalized medicine. Machine learning algorithms can analyze vast amounts of patient data to identify patterns and predict patient outcomes, leading to more accurate diagnoses and targeted treatments. AI-powered chatbots and virtual assistants are also revolutionizing patient engagement, providing instant access to health information and support.

AI is transforming the financial industry by improving risk assessment, fraud detection, and customer service. AI-driven algorithms can analyze large datasets to make more informed investment decisions and predict market trends. Additionally, natural language processing and machine learning technologies are powering chatbots and virtual assistants that provide real-time, personalized financial advice to customers.

In the retail and e-commerce sectors, AI is enhancing customer experiences through personalized product recommendations and targeted marketing. AI-powered inventory management and pricing algorithms can optimize supply chains and maximize profits. Furthermore, AI-enabled logistics systems are improving delivery times and efficiency, reducing costs for both businesses and consumers.

The impact of AI on the global economy and businesses is undeniable, and its influence will only continue to grow as technology advances. The key to harnessing AI's potential lies in understanding its capabilities, identifying opportunities for its application, and adapting to the evolving landscape. Companies and individuals who can do this will be well-positioned to thrive in the AI-driven economy.

Wealth Creation through AI in Personal Finance

The potential for wealth creation using AI is immense, beginning with personal finance. AI-powered robo-advisors, for instance, are revolutionizing the way individuals manage their investments. These platforms use advanced algorithms to assess risk tolerance, investment horizon, and financial goals, enabling them to provide personalized investment strategies. By automating the investment process, individuals can optimize their portfolios, reduce costs, and ultimately, increase their wealth.

AI is also powering a new generation of personal finance management apps, which provide insights into spending habits, help set budgets, and automate savings. By leveraging AI, these apps can predict future income and expenses, help avoid unnecessary fees, and even suggest ways to save money, contributing to wealth accumulation over time.

AI and the Stock Market

In the stock market, AI has the potential to generate significant wealth. AI-powered algorithms are used in high-frequency trading, where they analyze massive volumes of data and execute trades in milliseconds, capturing opportunities that would be impossible for human traders. Similarly, AI can be used to analyze market sentiment, predict stock price movements, and provide actionable investment insights, potentially leading to increased returns.

Real Estate and AI

AI is also transforming the real estate sector, a traditional avenue for wealth creation. AI-powered platforms can analyze vast amounts of data on property prices, location characteristics, market trends, and more, enabling more informed investment decisions. Additionally, AI can automate various aspects of property management, including tenant screening, rent collection, and maintenance requests, leading to cost savings and increased returns on investment.

AI in E-Commerce and Retail

E-commerce and retail businesses can use AI to drive revenue growth and maximize profitability, leading to wealth creation. AI can personalize customer experiences by providing tailored product recommendations, enhancing customer engagement, and driving sales. Moreover, AI can optimize inventory management, pricing strategies, and logistics, improving operational efficiency and bottom-line performance.

AI as a Service (AIaaS)

There's also considerable potential for wealth creation in AI as a Service (AIaaS). As AI technologies continue to evolve, there's a growing demand for AI solutions across industries. By developing and offering AI services - such as AI-powered analytics, chatbots, and machine learning models - businesses and entrepreneurs can tap into a lucrative market.

Intellectual Property and AI

Finally, AI can generate wealth through the creation and licensing of intellectual property. AI algorithms can create unique content, designs, and inventions, which can be protected and licensed, creating a new revenue stream.

In conclusion, AI is a powerful tool for wealth creation, offering opportunities across a wide range of sectors. By leveraging AI, individuals and businesses can optimize their financial strategies, unlock new revenue streams, and ultimately, increase their wealth.

Overview of the 45 AI Strategies

The 45 strategies presented in this book cover a vast array of sectors and opportunities where AI can be leveraged for wealth creation. Each strategy provides insights into how AI is revolutionizing these sectors and how you can capitalize on these changes to build wealth. Here is a brief overview of what you can expect.

AI for Personal Finance

In the personal finance domain, we'll explore how AI can help in managing your finances more effectively, including AI-driven investment platforms, robo-advisors for portfolio management, and AI-aided personal finance management tools. These strategies will delve into how AI can help you make better financial decisions, save more, and invest wisely.

AI in the Stock Market

When it comes to the stock market, AI has brought about a new era of high-speed and high-frequency trading. We will look into strategies involving AI-powered stock analysis and prediction, portfolio optimization using AI, and even AI-driven sentiment analysis for investment decisions.

AI in Real Estate

In the realm of real estate, we'll discuss how AI can revolutionize property valuation, investment analysis, and even property management. From AI-based property valuation and predictions to AI-powered real estate marketing platforms, you will learn how AI can transform real estate investments and management.

AI in E-commerce

In the e-commerce sector, we'll explore how AI can help businesses deliver better customer experiences, streamline operations, and maximize profits. Strategies here will include AI-powered product recommendation engines, AI-driven pricing and inventory management, and the use of chatbots for customer support.

AI as a Service (AIaaS)

We'll also delve into the rapidly growing field of AI as a Service (AIaaS). Here, you'll learn how to identify market needs and offer AI solutions, build and monetize AI models, and provide AI consulting and strategy development services.

AI in Content Creation

The content creation sector is another area where AI is making a significant impact. Strategies in this area will include the use of AI-powered content generation tools, AI-driven video and image editing, and personalized content recommendations and curation using AI.

AI for Intellectual Property and Licensing

We'll also explore how AI can be used to create and license intellectual property. Strategies here will cover creating and licensing AI-generated content, AI-driven patent analysis and valuation, and AI-based copyright protection and enforcement.

AI for Startups and Entrepreneurship

Finally, we'll examine how AI can drive startups and entrepreneurship. This includes AI-driven market research and validation, building and scaling AI-powered startups, and securing funding and investments for AI-focused ventures.

Each of these strategies provides an opportunity to harness the power of AI for wealth creation. By understanding and applying these strategies, you can position yourself at the forefront of the AI revolution, ready to unlock your path to financial freedom.

Understanding the Basics of AI

To get started with AI, you first need to understand its basics. AI, or Artificial Intelligence, refers to the ability of a computer system or machine to mimic human intelligence—learning from experiences, adjusting to new inputs, and performing tasks that typically require human intellect. AI can be classified into two main types: narrow AI, which is designed to perform a specific task, such as voice recognition, and general AI, which can perform any intellectual task that a human being can do.

Machine Learning (ML), a subset of AI, involves algorithms that improve automatically through experience. It uses statistical methods to enable machines to improve with experience. Deep Learning, a subfield of ML, imitates the working of the human brain in processing data for decision making. Understanding these concepts is crucial to grasp the potential of AI and how it can be leveraged for wealth creation.

Identifying AI Opportunities in Various Industries

Once you have a basic understanding of AI, the next step is identifying opportunities where AI can be applied. As discussed in the overview of the 45 strategies, AI has permeated virtually every industry, from finance and healthcare to manufacturing and retail. It is being used for a variety of applications, such as personalizing customer experiences, automating processes, making predictions, and generating insights from data. Identifying these opportunities requires an understanding of your own skills, interests, and resources, as well as a keen awareness of industry trends and developments.

Developing an AI-Focused Mindset

Developing an AI-focused mindset is another essential step in getting started with AI. This involves embracing a data-driven approach to decision-making, being open to new technologies and ways of doing things, and continually learning and adapting. It also involves understanding the ethical implications of AI and considering issues such as privacy and bias in AI algorithms.

An AI-focused mindset is not just about using AI tools and technologies; it's also about thinking in terms of AI. This means viewing problems and opportunities from an AI perspective and considering how AI could be used to solve problems, improve efficiency, or create new products or services.

Learning AI Skills and Tools

While you don't need to be a computer scientist to leverage AI for wealth creation, having some basic AI skills can be beneficial. There are numerous online courses and resources that can help you learn about AI, machine learning, and related topics. You may also want to familiarize yourself with some of the tools used in AI, such as Python programming language, TensorFlow, and other machine learning libraries.

Creating an AI Strategy

Finally, getting started with AI involves creating an AI strategy. This includes defining your AI goals, identifying the resources you need, developing a plan for implementing AI in your activities, and measuring your progress. An effective AI strategy will guide your AI journey, helping you to focus your efforts and maximize your results.

In conclusion, getting started with AI involves understanding the basics of AI, identifying AI opportunities, developing an AI-focused mindset, learning AI skills and tools, and creating an AI strategy. By taking these steps, you can position yourself to leverage the power of AI for wealth creation.

Understanding Artificial Intelligence

Artificial Intelligence (AI) represents a branch of computer science that aims to create systems capable of performing tasks that would normally require human intelligence. These tasks include learning from experience, understanding natural language, recognizing patterns, solving problems, and making decisions. The concept of AI is based on the idea of building machines capable of thinking, learning, and acting like humans.

AI can be categorized into two types: Narrow AI and General AI. Narrow AI, also known as weak AI, is designed to perform a specific task, such as voice recognition or driving a car. It operates under a limited context and is a simulation of human intelligence. On the other hand, General AI, also known as strong AI, exhibits all aspects of human intelligence, including the capacities to understand, learn, adapt, and implement knowledge in different domains. As of now, General AI remains largely theoretical, with no practical examples in use.

Machine Learning: A Key Subset of AI

An essential part of understanding AI is understanding Machine Learning (ML). ML is a subset of AI that involves the practice of using algorithms to parse data, learn from it, and then make a prediction or decision about something in the world. Instead of hand-coding software routines with a specific set of instructions to accomplish a task, the machine is "trained" using large amounts of data and algorithms that give it the ability to learn how to perform the task.

There are several types of machine learning, including supervised learning, unsupervised learning, semi-supervised learning, and reinforcement learning. Each type has its strengths and weaknesses and is used for different types of tasks and applications.

Deep Learning: Going Deeper into AI

Deep Learning, a further subset of machine learning, is another vital concept in understanding AI. It mimics the workings of the human brain in processing data for use in decision making. Deep learning algorithms, also known as artificial neural networks, are designed to recognize patterns. They interpret sensory data through a kind of machine perception, labeling or clustering raw input.

These algorithms can recognize patterns with an accuracy that often surpasses human capability. They have been used for various practical applications, including voice control in consumer devices, language translation, and identifying complex patterns in vast amounts of data.

Natural Language Processing: Making Machines Understand Us

Natural Language Processing (NLP) is another key facet of AI. NLP is the technology used to aid computers to understand the human's natural language. It involves machine interpretation, generation, and understanding of human language. This leads to the development of interfaces that can understand and respond to human language, thus enabling humans to interact with computers in natural human terms.

Understanding the basics of AI is the first step to unlocking its potential for various applications, including wealth creation. As AI continues to evolve, it is fundamentally altering the way we live and work, offering numerous opportunities for those who understand and can apply this powerful technology.

Identifying AI opportunities in various industries

AI in Healthcare

AI offers numerous opportunities in the healthcare industry, with applications ranging from diagnostics to patient care and administrative tasks. Machine learning algorithms can analyze vast amounts of patient data to predict outcomes, identify disease patterns, and guide treatment plans. AI-powered chatbots and virtual health assistants provide round-the-clock patient support, while AI algorithms help in drug discovery and personalized medicine. Furthermore, AI can automate administrative tasks like appointment scheduling, billing, and maintaining patient records, freeing up time for healthcare providers to focus on patient care.

AI in Finance

In the finance sector, AI is transforming processes and service delivery. Robo-advisors offer personalized investment advice, while AI algorithms are used in high-frequency trading, making predictions based on large datasets and executing trades in fractions of a second. AI is also used for risk assessment, fraud detection, and to improve customer service. AI-powered chatbots answer customer queries in real-time, and machine learning algorithms analyze customer data to offer personalized financial products.

AI in Manufacturing

The manufacturing sector is reaping the benefits of AI in improving efficiency and productivity. Smart factories leverage AI technologies for predictive maintenance, where AI algorithms predict machine failures and schedule maintenance, reducing downtime. AI-powered quality control systems automatically detect defects in products, improving accuracy and reducing waste. Additionally, AI is used in supply chain management, optimizing inventory levels and improving logistics.

AI in Retail and E-commerce

AI is revolutionizing the retail and e-commerce sectors by enhancing the customer experience and streamlining operations. AI-powered recommendation engines offer personalized product suggestions based on customer preferences and shopping behavior. AI chatbots provide customer support, while AI algorithms manage inventory and predict demand. AI is also used in dynamic pricing, where prices are adjusted in real-time based on factors like demand, competition, and customer behavior.

AI in Education

In education, AI is transforming teaching and learning. AI-powered adaptive learning systems offer personalized learning experiences, adjusting content and delivery based on a student's progress and learning style. AI is also used in administrative tasks, automating processes like admissions, scheduling, and grading. Furthermore, AI chatbots answer student queries, and AI algorithms analyze student data to predict outcomes and identify areas for improvement.

AI in Transportation and Logistics

In transportation and logistics, AI is used to optimize routes, predict delivery times, and manage fleets. AI-powered autonomous vehicles promise to revolutionize transport, while AI algorithms improve logistics efficiency by optimizing routes and managing inventories. In supply chain management, AI is used to predict demand and optimize inventory levels, reducing costs and improving efficiency.

These examples illustrate the vast opportunities for AI across various industries. The potential applications of AI are only limited by our imagination. By identifying these opportunities, individuals and businesses can leverage AI to drive growth, improve efficiency, and create value

Embracing a Data-Driven Approach

Developing an AI-focused mindset starts with embracing a data-driven approach. AI thrives on data; the more quality data it has, the better it performs. This means that to successfully use AI, you must learn to value data and use it to drive decisions. This involves gathering and analyzing data, using it to generate insights, and making decisions based on those insights rather than just relying on intuition or experience. A data-driven mindset also involves understanding the importance of data quality and investing in data management and governance.

Continuous Learning and Adaptability

AI is a rapidly evolving field, with new advancements, tools, and applications emerging all the time. As such, an AI-focused mindset involves continuous learning and adaptability. You need to stay updated with the latest AI trends, technologies, and best practices, and be willing to continually update your skills and knowledge. This might involve taking online courses, attending AI conferences and seminars, reading AI research papers, or participating in AI communities and forums. Adaptability also involves being open to changing your strategies or approaches based on new information or insights.

Understanding the Ethical Implications of AI

AI is not just about technology; it also has significant ethical implications. These include issues related to privacy, bias, transparency, and accountability. An AI-focused mindset involves understanding these ethical issues and considering them in your AI strategies and initiatives. This might involve developing ethical guidelines for AI use, implementing measures to prevent bias in AI algorithms, or ensuring transparency in how AI systems make decisions.

Problem-Solving and Creativity

AI is a powerful tool for solving problems and generating new ideas. Therefore, an AI-focused mindset involves using AI to approach problems in new ways, find innovative solutions, and create new products, services, or business models. This involves thinking critically about how AI can be applied to address challenges or opportunities, and being creative in designing AI solutions.

Collaboration and Communication

Finally, an AI-focused mindset involves collaboration and communication. AI is a multidisciplinary field that involves various stakeholders, including data scientists, business leaders, IT professionals, and end-users. As such, you need to be able to collaborate with different teams and individuals, understand their perspectives, and communicate effectively about AI. This involves explaining complex AI concepts in simple terms, advocating for AI initiatives, and building consensus around AI strategies and decisions.

In conclusion, developing an AI-focused mindset is a crucial step in leveraging AI effectively. This involves embracing a data-driven approach, committing to continuous learning and adaptability, understanding the ethical implications of AI, using AI for problem-solving and creativity, and fostering collaboration and communication. By adopting this mindset, you can maximize the benefits of AI and drive successful AI initiatives.

AI in Personal Finance Management

AI has brought significant advancements to personal finance management. Today, various AI-powered applications can analyze spending habits, track expenses, and provide personalized advice on budgeting and saving money. By leveraging machine learning algorithms, these applications can learn from your financial behavior, provide insights into your spending patterns, and even predict future expenses. This helps users gain a better understanding of their financial habits and make informed decisions about their money.

AI in Investment and Portfolio Management

AI has been a game-changer in the investment industry, particularly in portfolio management. Robo-advisors, powered by AI algorithms, are now commonplace. These digital platforms provide automated, algorithm-driven financial planning services with little to no human supervision. A typical robo-advisor collects information from clients about their financial situation and future goals through an online survey, and then uses the data to offer advice and automatically invest client assets.

Robo-advisors can manage portfolios more efficiently than humans can, analyzing a vast number of investment options and optimizing portfolios based on various factors such as risk tolerance, investment horizon, and specific financial goals. These platforms can rebalance portfolios automatically, ensuring that your investments stay aligned with your goals.

AI in Predicting Market Trends

Predicting market trends is another area where AI has shown significant potential. AI-powered systems can analyze vast amounts of financial data, including historical prices, economic indicators, and news articles, to make predictions about future market movements. These predictions can be used to guide investment decisions and develop trading strategies.

Moreover, AI can also help in predicting personal financial needs. For instance, it can predict when you might need a loan or face a cash crunch based on your financial habits, enabling you to plan ahead and manage your finances more effectively.

AI in Financial Planning

AI is also being used in financial planning, helping individuals plan for their financial future. AI systems can analyze a variety of data, including income, expenses, financial goals, and market trends, to create personalized financial plans. These plans can cover various aspects of financial planning, including budgeting, saving, investing, retirement planning, and tax planning.

Furthermore, AI can also monitor your progress towards your financial goals and adjust your financial plan as needed. For instance, if your income increases, an AI system might suggest increasing your savings or investments. If you're falling behind on your retirement savings, it might suggest ways to catch up.

AI in Insurance

AI has also found its place in the insurance industry. AI-powered applications can analyze various data to provide personalized insurance products. They can also process claims faster and more accurately, improving customer experience and reducing costs for insurance companies.

In conclusion, AI is transforming personal finance in numerous ways, making it easier for individuals to manage their money, make investments, plan for their financial future, and get insurance. By leveraging AI, you can gain better control over your finances, make smarter financial decisions, and work more effectively towards your financial goals

Robo-advisors for portfolio management

AI-driven investment platforms, often referred to as robo-advisors, have gained significant popularity over the past few years. They leverage AI and machine learning algorithms to provide automated, personalized investment advice and manage client portfolios with minimal human intervention. Here are some key ways AI-driven investment platforms are shaping the investment landscape:

Automated Portfolio Management

One of the core features of AI-driven investment platforms is automated portfolio management. Upon signing up, users answer a series of questions about their investment goals, risk tolerance, and time horizon. The AI algorithms then analyze these inputs to create a diversified portfolio tailored to the user's specific needs. These portfolios often consist of low-cost exchange-traded funds (ETFs) spread across different asset classes to maximize returns and minimize risk.

Dynamic Portfolio Rebalancing

AI-driven investment platforms automatically rebalance portfolios to ensure they remain aligned with the investor's goals. For instance, if the stock portion of a portfolio outperforms the bond portion, leading to a higher risk profile than intended, the platform can sell some stocks and buy bonds to restore the original balance. This automated rebalancing eliminates the need for investors to monitor and adjust their portfolios manually.

Tax-Loss Harvesting

Some AI-driven investment platforms offer tax-loss harvesting, a strategy that involves selling securities at a loss to offset capital gains tax liability. AI algorithms can identify opportunities for tax-loss harvesting and execute trades automatically, helping investors reduce their tax bills and boost after-tax returns.

Personalized Investment Advice

AI-driven investment platforms provide personalized investment advice based on the user's financial situation and goals. They can recommend strategies for retirement savings, college savings, buying a home, and other financial goals. Moreover, some platforms offer AI-powered financial planning tools that can simulate different scenarios and help investors understand how their decisions might impact their financial future.

Market Predictions and Risk Assessment

AI-driven investment platforms can analyze vast amounts of financial data, including historical price trends, economic indicators, and news articles, to predict market trends and assess investment risks. These insights can inform investment decisions and help investors navigate market volatility.

Ease of Use and Accessibility

AI-driven investment platforms are typically user-friendly and accessible, making investing more approachable for beginners. They allow investors to start investing with small amounts of money, and they charge lower fees than traditional investment advisors.

In conclusion, AI-driven investment platforms are democratizing investing by making it more accessible, personalized, and efficient. They are an excellent option for both novice and experienced investors who want a hands-off approach to investing. However, like all investment strategies, they come with risks, and it's crucial for investors to do their due diligence and understand the potential risks before investing.

Robo-advisors have emerged as a popular tool for portfolio management, particularly among the younger generation and novice investors. They offer a unique blend of automation, customization, and low costs, making them an appealing alternative to traditional financial advisors. Here's a detailed look at how robo-advisors function in the realm of portfolio management:

Personal finance management using AI

Automated Portfolio Creation and Management

When you sign up for a robo-advisor service, you're usually prompted to complete a questionnaire. This typically covers your financial goals, risk tolerance, and investment timeline. Using algorithms, the robo-advisor processes your responses and automatically constructs a portfolio aligned with your investment profile. The portfolio is generally composed of a diversified mix of asset classes, often represented by low-cost exchange-traded funds (ETFs).

Dynamic Rebalancing

One of the key features of robo-advisors is their ability to dynamically rebalance portfolios. Rebalancing involves adjusting the proportions of different assets in a portfolio to maintain an intended level of risk and return. If one asset class outperforms others and becomes a larger part of the portfolio, rebalancing would entail selling some of that asset and buying more of others to restore the original asset allocation. Robo-advisors do this automatically, ensuring that the portfolio remains aligned with the investor's risk tolerance and investment goals.

Tax Optimization

Many robo-advisors offer tax optimization strategies, such as tax-loss harvesting. This strategy involves selling investments that have declined in value to offset capital gains taxes on investments that have performed well. This process, managed by the robo-advisor, can enhance net returns and make the investment process more tax-efficient.

Cost Efficiency

Robo-advisors generally charge lower fees than traditional human advisors, making them an attractive option for cost-conscious investors. By automating processes and reducing the need for human intervention, robo-advisors can offer portfolio management services at a fraction of the cost of traditional financial advisors.

Accessibility and Convenience

Robo-advisors offer easy access and convenience. They are typically available 24/7 and can be accessed from anywhere with an internet connection. This flexibility allows investors to review their portfolios, make changes, or check on their investment performance at their convenience.

Caveats

While robo-advisors offer many benefits, they may not be suitable for everyone. They often work best for straightforward investment scenarios and may not be able to handle complex financial planning needs. Additionally, while their algorithms are sophisticated, they can't fully replicate the personal touch or subjective judgement of a human advisor.

In conclusion, robo-advisors represent a significant innovation in portfolio management, making it more accessible, affordable, and efficient. However, as with any investment tool, potential users should carefully consider their individual needs and circumstances before choosing to invest with a robo-advisor.

Artificial Intelligence (AI) has significantly transformed personal finance management, making it more convenient, efficient, and personalized. By leveraging machine learning and data analysis, AI tools can offer insights, predictions, and automated services that were previously unimaginable. Here's how AI is shaping personal finance management:

Expense Tracking and Budgeting

AI-powered apps can automatically track your spending across various categories, such as groceries, utilities, dining out, and more. By analyzing your spending habits, these apps can provide insights into where your money is going and identify areas where you could potentially save. They can also help you create and manage a budget, sending alerts when you're close to exceeding your budget or when unusual spending is detected.

Savings and Investment

AI can automate savings by analyzing your income, expenses, and spending habits to determine a safe amount to save each month. Some apps can even round up your purchases to the nearest dollar and transfer the difference to your savings account.

When it comes to investments, AI-powered robo-advisors can manage your portfolio, adjusting investments based on market trends and your personal risk tolerance. These platforms can offer personalized investment advice and automatically rebalance your portfolio as needed.

Debt Management and Credit Score Improvement

AI can also help manage debts more effectively. By analyzing your income, expenses, interest rates, and repayment schedules, AI tools can suggest the best strategies for paying off your debts. They can also provide recommendations for improving your credit score, such as reducing your credit utilization or fixing errors in your credit report.

Personalized Financial Advice

Perhaps one of the most promising applications of AI in personal finance is the provision of personalized financial advice. AI tools can analyze your financial situation, goals, and habits to provide tailored advice. This can include recommendations for saving money, investing, retirement planning, tax planning, and more. Some tools can even simulate different scenarios to help you understand the potential outcomes of different financial decisions.

Fraud Detection and Security

AI is also used to enhance the security of financial transactions. Machine learning algorithms can identify patterns and anomalies in transaction data that might indicate fraudulent activity. If unusual activity is detected, the system can alert the user or even block the transaction to prevent fraud.

In conclusion, AI is revolutionizing personal finance management by automating tedious tasks, providing personalized advice, and enhancing security. However, while AI tools can be incredibly helpful, it's important to remember that they are tools and not a substitute for a comprehensive financial plan.

It's always advisable to consult with a financial advisor or conduct your own research before making major financial decisions.

Automated savings and budgeting tools

Automated savings and budgeting tools have become increasingly popular in recent years, with advancements in AI and machine learning playing a significant role in their development. Here are some ways these tools are helping individuals manage their finances more effectively:

Automated Savings

One of the key features of automated savings tools is the ability to automatically transfer funds from a checking account to a savings account. Users can set the amount and frequency of these transfers based on their comfort level. Some apps even offer features like "round-up" savings, where purchases are rounded up to the nearest dollar and the difference is saved.

In addition, some tools use AI to analyze a user's income, expenses, and spending habits to determine an optimal amount to save each month. The tool can then automatically transfer this amount to a savings account, helping the user save money without having to think about it.

Automated Budgeting

Automated budgeting tools can help users create and manage a budget more effectively. They can automatically categorize transactions, track expenses, and provide a real-time view of spending against the budget. If the user is close to exceeding the budget in a particular category, the tool can send an alert to help prevent overspending.

These tools can also use AI to analyze spending habits and provide insights and recommendations. For instance, if the tool notices that a user spends a lot on dining out, it might suggest cooking at home more often to save money.

Goal Tracking and Progress

Many automated savings and budgeting tools allow users to set financial goals, such as saving for a vacation or paying off a debt. The tool can track the user's progress towards these goals and provide updates and motivation. Some tools can even suggest changes to the budget or savings plan to help the user achieve their goals faster.

Financial Insights and Advice

Some advanced tools use AI to provide personalized financial insights and advice. They can analyze a user's financial situation, goals, and habits to provide recommendations for saving money, reducing expenses, or improving financial habits.

In conclusion, automated savings and budgeting tools can help individuals manage their finances more effectively by automating tedious tasks, providing real-time insights and alerts, and offering personalized advice. However, while these tools can be incredibly helpful, they are not a substitute for a comprehensive financial plan or professional financial advice. It's always important to understand your financial situation and goals, and to consult with a financial advisor if needed.

AI in the Stock Market

Algorithmic trading and high-frequency trading

One of the most prominent applications of AI in the stock market is algorithmic trading, also known as algo-trading or black-box trading. Algorithmic trading uses complex AI systems to make high-speed trading decisions. These systems can analyze market data, identify trading opportunities, and execute trades at a speed and accuracy level that is beyond human capability.

These AI systems can analyze various factors, such as price, timing, volume, and even news headlines, to make predictions about stock price movements and execute trades accordingly. This process involves the use of high-frequency trading algorithms that can execute thousands of trades in a fraction of a second, often resulting in significant profits.

AI and Predictive Analytics

AI has revolutionized predictive analytics in the stock market. Predictive analytics involves using historical and current data to forecast future events. In the context of the stock market, predictive analytics can be used to predict future price movements, volatility, trading volume, and other important market indicators.

AI systems, particularly those that use machine learning, are exceptionally good at predictive analytics. They can analyze vast amounts of data, identify patterns, and make accurate predictions. These predictions can be used to inform trading decisions and investment strategies, giving traders and investors an edge in the market.

AI and Sentiment Analysis

Sentiment analysis, also known as opinion mining, involves analyzing social media posts, news articles, and other text data to gauge public sentiment towards a particular stock or the stock market as a whole. This information can provide valuable insights into market trends and can be used to predict stock price movements.

AI has significantly improved the accuracy and efficiency of sentiment analysis. Natural Language Processing (NLP), a subfield of AI, enables machines to understand and interpret human language. AI systems can use NLP to analyze vast amounts of text data, identify positive or negative sentiment, and provide real-time insights into market sentiment.

AI and Risk Management

Risk management is a crucial aspect of trading and investing in the stock market. AI systems can analyze a wide range of data, including market trends, economic indicators, and company financials, to assess the risk associated with a particular investment. These systems can also monitor a portfolio's risk level in real-time and suggest adjustments to mitigate risk and optimize returns.

AI and Personalized Investment Service

AI is being used to create personalized investment services, such as robo-advisors. These services use AI algorithms to provide personalized investment advice and manage client portfolios with minimal human intervention. Based on the client's financial goals, risk tolerance, and investment horizon, the robo-advisor creates a diversified portfolio and automatically rebalances it as needed.

In conclusion, AI is transforming the stock market in numerous ways, making trading and investing more efficient, accurate, and personalized. However, like all investment strategies, those involving AI also come with risks. It's important for traders and investors to understand these risks and use AI tools responsibly.

Algorithmic Trading

Algorithmic trading, also known as algo-trading or automated trading, involves the use of computer algorithms and complex mathematical models to make high-speed trading decisions. This form of trading has grown exponentially in recent years, largely due to advancements in technology and the increased availability of data.

The algorithms used in algo-trading are designed to execute a variety of tasks, including market making, inter-market spreading, arbitrage, or speculation. They take into account a variety of factors, such as price, volume, time, and even real-time news events, to make trading decisions.

The benefits of algorithmic trading are numerous. Firstly, it eliminates the potential for human error in trading decisions, as trades are executed based on pre-defined criteria. Secondly, it allows for trades to be executed at the best possible prices, and it can even time trades to get the best possible deal. Finally, algorithmic trading is swift and efficient, allowing for a higher volume of trades per day than a human trader could achieve.

However, algorithmic trading is not without its risks. If an algorithm is based on flawed logic or if it interprets market conditions incorrectly, it can lead to significant losses. Moreover, the use of algorithmic trading can lead to market volatility if many algorithms react to the same market conditions in a similar manner.

High-Frequency Trading (HFT)

High-frequency trading (HFT) is a type of algorithmic trading characterized by high speeds, high turnover rates, and high order-to-trade ratios. HFT firms leverage sophisticated technologies to trade large volumes of securities in fractions of a second.

HFT strategies are primarily focused on speed. They rely on ultra-fast data feeds and high-speed connections to execute trades at a pace that would be impossible for human traders. The goal is to capitalize on minute discrepancies in stock prices and trade volumes.

In terms of benefits, HFT can lead to greater market liquidity and efficiency. By rapidly buying and selling securities, high-frequency traders can help to reduce bid-ask spreads, making it easier for other market participants to trade.

However, like algorithmic trading, HFT is not without its critics. Some argue that high-frequency trading can contribute to market instability. For example, if many HFT algorithms react to a particular market event, they could exacerbate price volatility. Furthermore, there are concerns that HFT firms have unfair advantages over other market participants due to their access to superior technology and resources.

In conclusion, both algorithmic trading and high-frequency trading represent significant advancements in the field of finance. They can offer numerous benefits, including increased trading efficiency and liquidity. However, they also present unique challenges and risks, which regulators and market participants must carefully consider.

AI-powered stock analysis and prediction

AI-powered stock analysis and prediction have gained significant traction in recent years, thanks to advancements in machine learning and data analysis capabilities. AI can process and analyze vast amounts of data at high speeds, making it highly useful for stock analysis and forecasting. Here's a closer look at how AI is being used in these areas:

Data Analysis and Pattern Recognition

One of the key ways AI is used in stock analysis is through data analysis and pattern recognition. Machine learning algorithms can process and analyze vast amounts of data, including historical stock prices, company financials, and macroeconomic data. By analyzing this data, AI systems can identify patterns and relationships that might not be immediately apparent to human analysts.

For example, an AI system might analyze a company's financial data and historical stock prices to identify patterns that signal potential future price movements. It could also analyze macroeconomic data to understand how factors like interest rates, inflation, and economic growth could impact the stock market.

Predictive Analytics

AI has significantly improved the accuracy and efficiency of predictive analytics in stock analysis. Predictive analytics involves using historical and current data to forecast future events. In the context of the stock market, predictive analytics can be used to predict future price movements, volatility, trading volume, and other important market indicators.

Machine learning algorithms are exceptionally good at predictive analytics. They can analyze vast amounts of data, identify patterns, and make accurate predictions. These predictions can be used to inform trading decisions and investment strategies, giving traders and investors an edge in the market.

Sentiment Analysis

AI can also be used for sentiment analysis, which involves analyzing social media posts, news articles, and other forms of text data to gauge public sentiment towards a particular stock or the overall market. This information can provide valuable insights into market trends and can be used to predict stock price movements.

Natural Language Processing (NLP), a subfield of AI, enables machines to understand and interpret human language. AI systems can use NLP to analyze vast amounts of text data, identify positive or negative sentiment, and provide real-time insights into market sentiment.

Risk Assessment

AI can also be used for risk assessment in stock analysis. By analyzing a wide range of data, including market trends, economic indicators, and company financials, AI systems can assess the risk associated with a particular investment. This can help traders and investors make more informed decisions and manage their risk more effectively.

In conclusion, AI has the potential to revolutionize stock analysis and prediction. It can process and analyze vast amounts of data, identify patterns and relationships, predict future events, and assess risk. However, like all tools, it's not infallible and should be used as part of a broader investment strategy. It's also important to remember that investing in the stock market always involves risk, and past performance is not indicative of future results.

Portfolio optimization using AI

Artificial Intelligence (AI) is revolutionizing various industries, and property management is no exception. From predictive maintenance to tenant communication and energy management, AI is enabling smarter, more efficient property management. Here's a closer look at how AI is transforming this sector:

Predictive Maintenance

One of the most significant applications of AI in property management is predictive maintenance. AI systems can analyze data from sensors and IoT devices installed in a property to predict when equipment, like HVAC systems or elevators, might need maintenance.

For instance, an AI system could monitor an HVAC system's performance, identify patterns and anomalies, and predict when it might fail. By identifying potential issues before they become serious problems, property managers can prevent costly downtime and improve tenant satisfaction.

Tenant Communication and Support

AI-powered chatbots and virtual assistants are increasingly being used in property management to enhance tenant communication and support. These AI tools can answer common questions, schedule appointments, and even handle complaints, providing 24/7 support to tenants.

For example, a tenant could use a chatbot to report a maintenance issue, and the chatbot could automatically schedule a repair appointment. This not only improves the tenant experience but also reduces the workload for property management staff.

Energy Management

AI can also be used for energy management in properties. By analyzing data from various sources, including weather forecasts, occupancy patterns, and energy usage history, AI systems can optimize a building's energy use.

For example, an AI system could adjust a building's heating, ventilation, and air conditioning (HVAC) system based on the forecasted weather and occupancy patterns, reducing energy waste and saving money.

Lease Management and Rent Pricing

AI can assist in lease management by analyzing market trends, local amenities, and historical data to optimize rent prices. It can also monitor lease agreements, send reminders about upcoming renewals, and even identify patterns that could indicate a tenant is likely to move out.

Security

AI is also being used to enhance security in properties. AI-powered surveillance systems can monitor video feeds in real-time, identify suspicious activity, and alert property managers or security staff. Facial recognition technology can also be used to control access to certain areas of a property.

Smart Home Features

AI is powering a new generation of smart home features that improve the tenant experience. This includes everything from smart thermostats that adjust the temperature based on a tenant's preferences and schedule, to smart appliances that can be controlled via a smartphone app.

In conclusion, AI offers a wide range of benefits for property management, from improved maintenance and communication to enhanced energy efficiency and security. As AI technology continues to advance, it's likely that its role in property management will continue to grow. However, it's important to remember that while AI can automate many tasks, it can't replace the human touch entirely. Property management is a people-focused business, and successful property managers will be those who can leverage AI to enhance, not replace, their interactions with tenants.

AI-driven sentiment analysis for investment decisions

Artificial Intelligence (AI) is transforming the real estate investment sector by providing sophisticated analysis and insights that were previously impossible or too time-consuming to obtain. Here's a closer look at how AI is being utilized in real estate investment analysis:

Market Analysis and Trends Prediction

AI algorithms are capable of analyzing vast amounts of data, including historical property prices, economic indicators, population trends, and even social media sentiment. This allows them to identify patterns and trends that can help investors make more informed decisions. For instance, an AI system might analyze population growth, employment rates, and rental yields in different areas to identify emerging real estate hotspots.

Furthermore, AI can use this data to make predictions about future market trends. For instance, it might analyze economic indicators and property market data to predict how property prices are likely to change in the future. This can provide investors with valuable insights and help them plan their investment strategies more effectively.

Property Valuation and Investment Returns

AI can also be used to provide more accurate property valuations. Traditional property valuations often rely on a limited set of data and can be subject to human error. In contrast, AI systems can analyze a much wider range of data, including property features, local amenities, crime rates, and even environmental factors, to provide a more accurate estimate of a property's value.

In addition to property valuations, AI can also help investors analyze potential investment returns. For instance, an AI system could use data on rental yields, property prices, and property management costs to calculate the potential return on investment for a rental property.

Risk Assessment

Investing in real estate involves risk, and AI can help investors assess and manage this risk more effectively. By analyzing a wide range of data, AI systems can identify potential risks that might impact an investment. For example, it could identify areas with high vacancy rates, declining property values, or economic instability.

Furthermore, AI can help investors manage their risk by providing more accurate forecasts and predictions. For instance, an AI system could forecast future rental yields, property price changes, or economic conditions, allowing investors to make more informed decisions and manage their risk more effectively.

Portfolio Optimization

For investors with multiple properties, AI can assist in portfolio optimization. By analyzing the performance of different properties and considering factors such as diversification, risk, and investment goals, AI systems can provide recommendations for portfolio adjustments. This could involve buying or selling properties or adjusting rental prices, among other strategies.

In conclusion, AI is transforming real estate investment analysis by providing more accurate valuations, better risk assessment, and sophisticated market analysis. As AI technology continues to advance, it's likely to become an increasingly important tool for real estate investors. However, while AI can provide valuable insights and analysis, it's important to remember that it's not infallible, and investors should always use it as part of a broader investment strategy.

AI-based property valuation and predictions

Artificial Intelligence (AI) has been a game-changer for the e-commerce industry, enabling businesses to enhance customer experience, streamline operations, and increase sales. Here's a closer look at how AI is being utilized in e-commerce:

Personalized Shopping Experiences

One of the key ways AI is used in e-commerce is to personalize the shopping experience. AI algorithms can analyze a customer's browsing history, past purchases, and other behaviors to understand their preferences and interests. This information can then be used to personalize product recommendations, making them more relevant and likely to result in a purchase.

For example, if a customer frequently buys organic products, an AI system could recommend other organic products they might be interested in. Or if a customer often buys clothing in a certain size, the system could highlight items available in that size.

Chatbots and Customer Service

AI-powered chatbots are another significant application of AI in e-commerce. These chatbots can handle a variety of customer service tasks, such as answering common questions, helping customers track their orders, and even assistng with returns or exchanges.

This not only improves the customer experience by providing instant, 24/7 support, but also reduces the workload for human customer service agents, allowing them to focus on more complex queries.

Predictive Analytics

AI can also be used for predictive analytics in e-commerce. By analyzing past sales data, customer behavior, and other information, AI systems can predict future trends, such as which products are likely to be popular in the coming months or when sales might peak.

These predictions can be used to inform a variety of business decisions, such as which products to stock up on, when to run sales or promotions, and how to adjust pricing strategies.

Inventory Management

AI can significantly improve inventory management in e-commerce. By analyzing sales data, trends, and other factors, AI systems can forecast demand for different products and suggest optimal inventory levels.

This can help e-commerce businesses avoid stockouts and overstocking, reducing costs and improving customer satisfaction.

Fraud Detection

Fraud is a significant concern in e-commerce, and AI can play a crucial role in detecting and preventing it. AI systems can analyze a variety of data, such as transaction history and customer behavior, to identify suspicious activities that might indicate fraud.

For instance, if a customer who normally makes small, infrequent purchases suddenly starts making large, frequent purchases, this could be flagged as potential fraud.

AI-Powered Search

AI can improve the search functionality on e-commerce websites. By understanding natural language queries and learning from past searches, AI can provide more accurate and relevant search results, making it easier for customers to find what they're looking for.

In conclusion, AI is transforming the e-commerce industry in numerous ways, from personalizing the shopping experience to streamlining operations and preventing fraud. As AI technology continues to advance, it's likely to play an increasingly important role in e-commerce.

AI-powered real estate marketing platforms

AI-powered product recommendation engines are a game-changer in the world of e-commerce and digital marketing. They allow businesses to provide personalized suggestions, creating a more engaging and relevant experience for customers. Here's how AI is being utilized in product recommendation engines:

Understanding Customer Preferences

The first step to making relevant product recommendations is understanding a customer's preferences. AI algorithms can analyze a variety of data, including a customer's browsing history, past purchases, and even their interactions with marketing emails or ads, to build a detailed profile of their interests, preferences, and buying behavior.

For example, if a customer often buys organic products or frequently browses items in the fitness category, the AI system could infer that they are interested in health and fitness. This information could then be used to recommend products that align with these interests.

Personalized Recommendations

Once the AI system understands a customer's preferences, it can use this information to make personalized product recommendations. This could involve suggesting products that are similar to ones the customer has bought or viewed in the past, or recommending products that other customers with similar preferences have liked.

For instance, if a customer has recently bought a pair of running shoes, the AI system might recommend other running gear, like fitness trackers or water bottles. Or if a customer frequently buys crime novels, the system might recommend new releases in the crime genre.

Dynamic Recommendations

One of the key advantages of AI-powered product recommendation engines is that they can provide dynamic recommendations. This means that the recommendations can change in real-time based on the customer's behavior.

For example, if a customer adds a pair of jeans to their shopping cart, the AI system could instantly recommend matching tops or accessories. This not only enhances the shopping experience for the customer but can also increase the average order value for the business.

Predictive Recommendations

AI can also be used to make predictive recommendations. By analyzing patterns in a customer's behavior and purchases, AI can predict what products they might be interested in the future.

For instance, if a customer frequently buys diapers and baby products, the AI system might predict that they have a young child and recommend relevant products for that age group.

Improving Over Time

One of the significant benefits of AI-powered product recommendation engines is that they can improve over time. The more data the AI system has to work with, the better its recommendations become.

Every interaction a customer has with the website, from the products they view to the purchases they make, provides valuable data that the AI system can learn from. This means that the recommendations will become more accurate and relevant as the customer continues to interact with the website.

In conclusion, AI-powered product recommendation engines can significantly enhance the shopping experience for customers, making it more personalized, engaging, and convenient. They can also increase sales and revenue for businesses by encouraging customers to buy more products and making it easier for them to find products they're interested in. As AI technology continues to advance, it's likely that these recommendation engines will become even more sophisticated and effective.

SMART PROPERTY MANAGEMENT USING AI

Artificial Intelligence (AI) is revolutionizing the way businesses manage their pricing strategies and inventory, enabling them to make more informed decisions, minimize losses, and maximize profits. Here's a closer look at how AI is being utilized in pricing and inventory management:

Dynamic Pricing

Dynamic pricing is a pricing strategy that involves adjusting prices in real-time based on factors such as demand, competition, and customer behavior. AI-powered algorithms can analyze vast amounts of data, including historical sales data, competitor pricing, and current market trends, to determine the optimal price for a product at any given time.

For instance, an AI-driven pricing system could increase the price of a popular product when demand is high, maximizing profits, and then lower the price when demand decreases, encouraging sales. This not only helps businesses optimize their pricing strategies but also improves the customer experience by ensuring that prices are always competitive.

Demand Forecasting

Accurate demand forecasting is crucial for effective inventory management, helping businesses to avoid stockouts and overstocking. AI can analyze historical sales data, as well as other factors such as seasonality, promotions, and market trends, to predict future demand for different products.

For example, an AI system could forecast that demand for winter coats is likely to increase as the temperature drops, allowing businesses to stock up on these items in advance. This not only ensures that they have sufficient inventory to meet customer demand but also reduces the risk of lost sales due to stockouts.

Inventory Optimization

AI can also help businesses optimize their inventory levels, ensuring that they have the right amount of stock at the right time. By analyzing factors such as lead times, carrying costs, and demand forecasts, AI systems can suggest optimal inventory levels for different products.

For instance, an AI system might recommend that a business maintains a higher inventory level for a product with a long lead time, reducing the risk of stockouts, and a lower inventory level for a product with a short lead time, minimizing carrying costs.

Price Optimization for Inventory Clearance

AI-driven pricing systems can also help businesses to clear excess inventory more effectively. By analyzing factors such as the age of the inventory, demand trends, and competitor pricing, AI systems can suggest optimal pricing strategies for clearance sales.

For example, an AI system might recommend that a business offers a larger discount on a product that has been in stock for a long time, encouraging customers to buy it and helping the business to clear excess inventory more quickly.

Real-time Inventory Management

Real-time inventory management is crucial for businesses, helping them to respond quickly to changes in demand and minimize losses. AI systems can monitor inventory levels in real-time, alerting businesses to potential stockouts or overstocking issues and suggesting appropriate actions, such as re-ordering products or adjusting pricing strategies.

In conclusion, AI-driven pricing and inventory management can help businesses optimize their pricing strategies, improve demand forecasting, and streamline inventory management processes. By leveraging AI technology, businesses can make more informed decisions, minimize losses, and maximize profits. As AI continues to advance, it's likely to play an increasingly important role in pricing and inventory management, providing businesses with even more sophisticated tools and insights.

AI-driven real estate investment analysis

Artificial Intelligence (AI) has become an essential tool in the world of marketing and advertising, enabling businesses to create personalized experiences for their customers and deliver highly targeted ads. Here's a closer look at how AI is being utilized in personalized marketing and advertising:

Customer Segmentation and Profiling

One of the critical applications of AI in personalized marketing and advertising is customer segmentation and profiling. AI algorithms can analyze vast amounts of customer data, including demographics, online behavior, and purchase history, to create detailed profiles of individual customers.

These profiles can be used to segment customers into different groups based on their preferences, interests, and behaviors. For instance, an AI system could identify a group of customers who are interested in environmentally friendly products or a group that frequently purchases luxury items.

Personalized Content and Offers

Once customers have been segmented into different groups, businesses can use AI to generate personalized content and offers tailored to each group's interests and preferences. This could include customizing email campaigns, creating targeted landing pages, or offering personalized discounts and promotions.

For example, an AI system might generate an email campaign for eco-conscious customers that highlights the company's commitment to sustainability and offers a special discount on environmentally friendly products.

Dynamic Ad Targeting

AI can be used to deliver highly targeted ads to individual customers based on their profiles and online behavior. For instance, an AI-powered advertising platform could analyze a user's browsing history to determine their interests and then target them with ads for products that align with those interests.

This not only increases the chances of the ad being relevant and engaging to the user but also helps businesses optimize their ad spend by focusing on customers who are most likely to be interested in their products.

Retargeting and Cross-Selling

AI can also be used to retarget customers who have previously shown interest in a product or service but have not yet made a purchase. By analyzing a customer's online behavior and interactions with the brand, AI systems can determine the optimal time and channel to retarget them with personalized ads or offers.

For example, if a customer has recently abandoned their shopping cart, an AI system might retarget them with an email offering a discount on the items they left behind.

Similarly, AI can be used for cross-selling by recommending complementary products to customers based on their purchase history. For instance, if a customer has recently bought a new smartphone, the AI system might recommend a phone case or screen protector.

Real-time Personalization

One of the key advantages of AI-powered marketing and advertising is the ability to provide real-time personalization. This means that content and offers can be adapted instantly based on a customer's behavior, ensuring that they're always relevant and engaging.

For example, if a customer clicks on a personalized ad for a specific product category, the AI system could instantly update their profile to reflect their interest in that category and tailor future ads and content accordingly.

In conclusion, AI-driven personalized marketing and advertising can significantly improve the customer experience by providing more relevant and engaging content and offers. It can also help businesses optimize their marketing efforts and ad spend by focusing on customers who are most likely to be interested in their products. As AI technology continues to advance, it's likely to play an increasingly important role in personalized marketing and advertising, providing businesses with even more sophisticated tools and insights.

AI as a Service (AIaaS)

Identifying market needs and offering AI solutions

What is AI as a Service?

AI as a Service refers to the delivery of AI capabilities through cloud-based platforms, enabling businesses to access and utilize AI technologies on a subscription basis. This model allows organizations to take advantage of AI's benefits without having to invest heavily in hardware, software, or expert personnel.

By offering AIaaS, providers can create scalable and customizable solutions that cater to the specific needs of different businesses, allowing them to incorporate AI into their operations with minimal upfront costs and ongoing maintenance requirements.

Key Benefits of AIaaS

- Cost Efficiency: AIaaS allows businesses to access AI capabilities without the need for significant upfront investments in infrastructure and personnel. By subscribing to AI services on a pay-as-you-go basis, companies can reduce their overall expenses and allocate resources more efficiently.

- Scalability: AIaaS platforms are designed to be easily scalable, allowing businesses to adjust their AI capabilities according to their needs. This flexibility enables companies to implement AI solutions at a pace that suits their growth and requirements.

- Rapid Deployment: AIaaS can be quickly deployed, enabling businesses to start utilizing AI technologies almost immediately. This rapid deployment can help organizations gain a competitive advantage by allowing them to implement AI-driven solutions faster than competitors who are developing AI capabilities in-house.

- Access to Expertise: AIaaS providers often have teams of AI experts and data scientists who can assist businesses in implementing and optimizing AI solutions. This access to expertise can help organizations overcome knowledge gaps and ensure that they are maximizing the potential of their AI investments.

Applications of AI as a Service

- Natural Language Processing (NLP): AIaaS platforms can provide NLP services, enabling businesses to analyze and understand human language in text form. This can be used for sentiment analysis, chatbot development, or document classification, among other applications.

- Image and Video Analysis: AIaaS providers can offer image and video analysis services, allowing businesses to analyze and interpret visual data. This can be useful for applications such as facial recognition, object detection, or even medical imaging analysis.

- Predictive Analytics: AIaaS can be used for predictive analytics, enabling businesses to forecast future trends and make data-driven decisions. This can be applied in various industries, such as finance, healthcare, and retail, to predict customer behavior, market trends, or even equipment maintenance needs.

- Machine Learning Model Development: AIaaS platforms often include tools and environments for developing, training, and deploying machine learning models. This allows businesses to create custom AI solutions tailored to their specific needs without having to invest in extensive in-house expertise.

- Recommendation Engines: AIaaS can be used to create recommendation engines, providing personalized product or content suggestions to customers based on their preferences and behavior. This can help businesses improve customer engagement, boost sales, and enhance the overall customer experience.

In conclusion, AI as a Service (AIaaS) offers businesses a cost-effective and scalable way to access and implement AI technologies. By leveraging AIaaS, organizations can rapidly deploy AI-driven solutions, gain access to expert knowledge, and focus on their core competencies, rather than investing in expensive infrastructure and personnel. As AI technology continues to advance and its adoption becomes more widespread, AIaaS is poised to become an increasingly important component of the business landscape.

Identifying market needs and offering Artificial Intelligence (AI) solutions is crucial for businesses to gain a competitive edge, increase operational efficiency, and foster innovation. With AI technology's versatility, it can be applied across industries to solve a myriad of challenges. Here's an exploration of how businesses can identify market needs and provide AI solutions:

Understanding the Market

The first step in identifying market needs is thorough market research. This involves understanding the industry, the customers, and the competition. Research should focus on identifying the common pain points that businesses or customers experience. These could be inefficiencies in certain processes, a lack of actionable insights from data, or challenges in customer engagement and personalization.

Surveys, focus groups, interviews, and case studies can all provide valuable insights into these needs. Additionally, businesses should stay updated on industry trends and technological advancements, as these can often highlight emerging market needs.

Identifying Opportunities for AI

Once market needs are identified, businesses must then determine how AI could help address these needs. This involves mapping the capabilities of AI to the identified needs. For instance, if a market need is better customer personalization, AI's capabilities in data analysis and predictive modeling can be used to tailor products and services to individual customer preferences.

On the other hand, if businesses in a certain industry are struggling with managing large volumes of data, AI's capabilities in data processing and analysis can be leveraged to offer efficient data management solutions. Similarly, for industries where decision-making is crucial, AI's predictive analytics can provide valuable insights for better decision-making.

Developing AI Solutions

Developing AI solutions involves a combination of AI expertise, industry knowledge, and a deep understanding of the specific market need. For instance, if an AI solution is being developed to improve customer service in the retail industry, it will involve integrating AI technologies like natural language processing for chatbots, machine learning for predicting customer behavior, and data analytics for personalizing the customer experience.

The development process should also involve regular testing and iterations based on feedback to ensure the solution is effectively addressing the market need. Additionally, ethical considerations such as data privacy and AI bias should also be factored into the development process.

Communicating the Value of AI Solutions

Once an AI solution has been developed, businesses must effectively communicate its value to the target market. This involves demonstrating how the solution addresses the identified need and provides a tangible benefit, such as cost savings, increased efficiency, or improved customer satisfaction.

Businesses can use case studies, demonstrations, and testimonials to showcase the effectiveness of their AI solutions. Additionally, they should also be prepared to provide support and education to help customers understand and effectively use the AI solution.

In conclusion, identifying market needs and offering AI solutions requires a deep understanding of the market, the capabilities of AI, and the specific needs of customers. By effectively identifying market needs and developing tailored AI solutions, businesses can provide immense value to their customers, differentiate themselves from competitors, and drive innovation in their industry.

Building and monetizing AI models

Building and monetizing Artificial Intelligence (AI) models can be a lucrative venture, providing companies with significant competitive advantages and new revenue streams. This process involves creating AI models that have practical applications, and then generating income from these models in a variety of ways. Here's an exploration of how to build and monetize AI models:

Building AI Models

The process of building AI models involves several steps:

- Problem Definition: Identify the problem that the AI model aims to solve. This could be anything from predicting customer churn to detecting fraudulent transactions.

- Data Collection and Preparation: Gather and prepare the data that the model will use to learn. This involves collecting relevant data, cleaning it to remove errors or inconsistencies, and preprocessing it into a suitable format for the AI model.

- Model Selection and Training: Choose an appropriate AI model for the problem and train it on the prepared data. This might involve selecting a pre-existing model or developing a custom one, depending on the problem's complexity and the available data.

- Model Evaluation and Tuning: Evaluate the performance of the trained model and tune it to improve its accuracy. This might involve adjusting the model's parameters, using different training methods, or adding more data.

- Deployment and Monitoring: Deploy the trained model into a production environment and monitor its performance. This involves integrating the model into the company's existing systems and continually monitoring and updating it to ensure it remains effective.

Monetizing AI Models

Once a valuable AI model has been developed, there are several ways to monetize it:

- Selling AIaaS (AI as a Service): Companies can provide their AI models as a service, allowing customers to access the model's capabilities without having to develop their own AI infrastructure. This typically involves customers paying a subscription fee to use the AI model via an API.

- Licensing the Model: The AI model can be licensed to other companies, allowing them to use the model within their own systems. This typically involves a licensing fee, which may be a one-time payment or recurring payments.

- Selling Insights: The AI model can be used to generate valuable insights, which can then be sold to customers. For example, a company might use an AI model to analyze customer behavior and then sell these insights to marketers.

- Creating AI-Driven Products or Services: The AI model can be used to create new products or services that are then sold to customers. For example, a company might use an AI model to create a personalized recommendation engine, which could then be sold to e-commerce sites.

- Improving Operational Efficiency: While this isn't direct monetization, AI models can save businesses significant money by improving operational efficiency. For instance, an AI model could optimize a company's supply chain, reducing costs and thus increasing profits.

- Advertising and Marketing: AI models can be used to enhance advertising and marketing campaigns, leading to increased sales. For instance, AI models can help create personalized marketing campaigns or optimize ad placements, leading to a higher return on investment.

In conclusion, building and monetizing AI models can be a valuable venture, but it requires careful planning, skilled AI expertise, and a clear understanding of market needs and opportunities. With the right approach, businesses can leverage AI models to create new revenue streams, gain competitive advantages, and drive innovation.

AI consulting and strategy development

AI consulting and strategy development involves providing guidance, expertise, and support to businesses looking to adopt or optimize artificial intelligence (AI) technologies in their operations. As AI becomes increasingly important for businesses to maintain a competitive edge, AI consultants play a crucial role in helping organizations navigate the complexities of AI implementation and maximize its potential. Here's an overview of AI consulting and strategy development:

Role of AI Consultants

AI consultants are experts in AI technologies, data science, and machine learning, with a deep understanding of the various AI tools and applications available in the market. They work closely with businesses to develop AI strategies tailored to the organization's goals and requirements. The primary roles of AI consultants include:

- Identifying AI Opportunities: AI consultants help businesses identify areas where AI can be utilized to improve operations, increase efficiency, or drive innovation. This involves assessing the organization's current processes, technologies, and data infrastructure to pinpoint potential AI applications.

- Developing AI Strategy: Once opportunities for AI implementation have been identified, AI consultants work with the organization to develop a comprehensive AI strategy. This includes outlining the AI goals, selecting appropriate technologies and tools, and defining the timeline and resources required for implementation.

- AI Implementation Support: AI consultants guide businesses through the AI implementation process, offering support in areas such as data preparation, model development, and integration with existing systems. They also provide training and resources to help the organization's team develop the necessary skills to manage and maintain the AI systems.

- Performance Evaluation and Optimization: AI consultants monitor the performance of AI systems, ensuring they meet the organization's goals and objectives. They also help businesses optimize AI models, fine-tune algorithms, and address any challenges or issues that arise during implementation.

- Ethics and Compliance: AI consultants advise businesses on ethical considerations, such as data privacy and algorithmic bias, and ensure that AI implementation complies with relevant regulations and industry standards.

Benefits of AI Consulting and Strategy Development

Businesses that invest in AI consulting and strategy development can benefit in several ways:

- ·Competitive Advantage: By leveraging AI technologies, businesses can gain a competitive advantage over their rivals through improved efficiency, cost savings, and better decision-making.

- Increased Innovation: AI can help businesses innovate by automating routine tasks, enabling employees to focus on higher-value work and fostering creativity.

- Risk Mitigation: AI consultants can help businesses avoid potential pitfalls and risks associated with AI implementation, such as data breaches or biased algorithms, by providing expert guidance and support throughout the process.

- Maximizing ROI: By developing a clear AI strategy and ensuring optimal implementation, businesses can maximize the return on investment (ROI) from their AI initiatives.

In conclusion, AI consulting and strategy development is an essential service for businesses looking to harness the power of AI. By partnering with AI consultants, organizations can effectively identify AI opportunities, develop tailored AI strategies, and navigate the complexities of AI implementation, ensuring they maximize the potential of AI to drive growth, innovation, and competitive advantage.

AI-driven software and tools for businesses

Artificial Intelligence (AI) has transformed the landscape of business operations, offering a range of software and tools that can improve efficiency, make better predictions, automate tasks, and provide insightful data analysis. Here's an overview of some key AI-driven software and tools for businesses:

- Customer Relationship Management (CRM) Systems: AI has revolutionized CRM systems like Salesforce, HubSpot, and Zoho CRM. AI capabilities can predict customer behavior, automate data entry, provide insights about customer interactions, and even recommend the best times to contact customers.

- Chatbots and Virtual Assistants: AI-powered chatbots and virtual assistants, such as IBM Watson Assistant or Google Dialogflow, can interact with customers 24/7, handling customer inquiries, booking appointments, or providing product information. They can significantly enhance customer experience and free up human resources.

- Predictive Analytics Tools: AI-powered predictive analytics tools, like RapidMiner, Alteryx, or DataRobot, can analyze large datasets and forecast future trends. These tools are particularly valuable for making strategic decisions in areas like sales, marketing, and supply chain management.

- AI in Marketing: Tools like Marketo and Adobe Sensei employ AI to provide personalized experiences to customers, automate content delivery, perform A/B testing, and offer insightful analytics to optimize marketing strategies.

- Robotic Process Automation (RPA): RPA tools, like UiPath, Automation Anywhere, and Blue Prism, use AI to automate repetitive, rule-based tasks, improving operational efficiency and allowing employees to focus on more complex tasks.

- AI in HR: AI-driven HR tools like Eightfold or Pymetrics can help automate recruitment processes, match candidates with job profiles, and even predict the future performance of potential hires.

- Cybersecurity Tools: AI-driven cybersecurity solutions, such as Dark-trace or CrowdStrike, can identify and respond to security threats more quickly and accurately than traditional security tools, protecting businesses from cyberattacks and data breaches.

- AI in Supply Chain: Tools like Llamasoft or ClearMetal employ AI to optimize supply chain and logistics processes, including demand forecasting, inventory management, and route optimization.

- AI in Finance: AI-driven tools like Kabbage or Kensho provide solutions for financial forecasting, risk management, portfolio optimization, and fraud detection.

- AI in Sales: AI-powered sales tools like Gong or Chorus.ai can analyze sales calls and meetings, providing insights to improve sales strategies and performance.

These AI-driven software and tools can provide immense value to businesses across various industries. They can help in making data-driven decisions, automate routine tasks, provide personalized customer experiences, and offer valuable insights, all of which can lead to increased efficiency and revenue growth. However, businesses should consider their specific needs, budget, and existing infrastructure when choosing the right AI tools.

AI-powered content generation tools

AI has significantly impacted content creation, fundamentally transforming how content is generated, distributed, and consumed. With the rise of Natural Language Processing (NLP) and Machine Learning (ML), AI can now create human-like text, automate the content creation process, and provide valuable insights to optimize content strategies. Here's an overview of how AI is being used in content creation:

- **Automated Content Generation:** AI can automatically generate content for a variety of purposes. For example, AI-powered tools like OpenAI's GPT-3, Quill, or Wordsmith can write articles, blogs, product descriptions, social media posts, and more based on certain inputs and parameters. This can significantly reduce the time and effort required to create content, especially for repetitive and data-heavy content like financial reports, product descriptions, or news updates.

- **Content Optimization:** AI can also help optimize content for better engagement and visibility. AI-powered SEO tools like MarketMuse or Clearscope can analyze search data and provide suggestions for keywords, headings, and content length to improve search engine rankings. Similarly, AI tools can optimize social media content by determining the best times to post or the most engaging types of content.

- **Personalized Content:** AI can personalize content for individual users based on their behavior, preferences, and past interactions. This can greatly enhance the user experience and increase engagement. For example, Netflix uses AI to personalize movie and show recommendations, while Amazon uses AI to personalize product recommendations.

- **Predictive Analytics:** AI can analyze large amounts of data to predict future trends and user behavior. This can inform content strategies, helping businesses create content that resonates with their audience and meets market demands.

- **Content Curation:** AI can automate the process of content curation, gathering and organizing relevant content from various sources. Tools like DrumUp or Curata can help businesses provide their audience with valuable content, while also supplementing their own content creation efforts.

- **Chatbots and Virtual Assistants:** AI-powered chatbots and virtual assistants can create interactive content, engaging users in real-time conversations. This can enhance customer service, drive engagement, and provide valuable insights about user needs and preferences.

- **Image and Video Creation:** AI is also transforming image and video content creation. Tools like DeepArt or Lumen5 can create visually stunning graphics and videos based on text inputs, while tools like D-ID or Deepfake can generate realistic human images or alter video content.

While AI can greatly enhance and streamline content creation, it's important to note that it doesn't replace human creativity. AI is most effective when used as a tool to support and augment human content creators, providing automation and insights, but relying on humans for strategy, creativity, and final editorial control.

AI-powered content generation tools use natural language processing (NLP) and machine learning (ML) algorithms to create human-like text automatically. These tools can help businesses save time and resources, streamline content creation processes, and generate content tailored to specific audiences. Here are some notable AI-powered content generation tools:

- **OpenAI's GPT-3:** GPT-3 (Generative Pre-trained Transformer 3) is an advanced language model developed by OpenAI. It can generate coherent, contextually accurate, and human-like text for a wide range of purposes, including articles, blog posts, social media content, and more.

- **Jarvis by Conversion.ai:** Jarvis is a popular AI content generation tool that uses GPT-3 to create content for various purposes, such as blog posts, ad copy, social media posts, and product descriptions. It also offers templates to help guide the content generation process.

- **Kuki.ai:** Kuki.ai is another GPT-3-based content generation tool that allows users to create a variety of content types, including articles, product descriptions, social media content, and more. It features a user-friendly interface and offers templates to simplify the content creation process.

- **Quill:** Quill is an AI-powered content generation tool that specializes in generating data-driven narratives. It's particularly useful for creating financial reports, news updates, and other content types that rely heavily on structured data.

- **Articoolo:** Articoolo is an AI content generator that creates short-form content such as blog posts, news articles, or product descriptions. Users can input a few keywords or a topic, and Articoolo generates a unique, coherent piece of content.

- **WordAi:** WordAi is an AI-powered tool that focuses on rewriting and paraphrasing existing content. It can automatically rewrite articles, making them unique and readable while maintaining the original meaning and context.

- **Lumen5:** Lumen5 is an AI-powered video content generation tool that can convert text articles into engaging videos. It automatically suggests relevant images, videos, and audio based on the text input, allowing users to create professional-quality video content quickly and easily.

- **Grammarly:** Although Grammarly is primarily known as an AI-powered grammar and spell checker, it also offers content generation features, such as sentence rephrasing and suggestions for more effective word choices.

These AI-powered content generation tools can be a valuable addition to any content creator's toolkit, automating and streamlining the content creation process. However, it's important to remember that AI-generated content may require human oversight and editing to ensure quality, coherence, and alignment with brand guidelines.

AI-driven video and image editing

Artificial Intelligence (AI) is revolutionizing the field of video and image editing, bringing capabilities that were once reserved for skilled professionals into the hands of everyday users. Here's an overview of how AI is being used in video and image editing:

AI in Video Editing:

- Automatic Video Editing: Tools like Magisto and Adobe Premiere Rush use AI to automate the video editing process. They can analyze footage, select the best parts, and even add effects, transitions, and music based on the content and mood of the video.

- Object Recognition and Tracking: AI can identify and track objects within a video, which can be useful for adding effects or making adjustments to specific elements within the frame. Tools like Adobe After Effects offer this feature.

- Video Enhancement: AI can enhance the quality of video footage, improving resolution, reducing noise, and correcting color. Tools like Topaz Video Enhance AI are capable of upscaling video resolution up to 8K.

- Deepfakes: AI can create realistic deepfakes - videos where the face of a person is replaced with someone else's. While this has raised ethical concerns, it also has potential uses in filmmaking and special effects. Tools like DeepFaceLab are used for this purpose.

AI in Image Editing:

- Automatic Image Editing: Tools like Luminar AI and Photoshop use AI to automate many image editing tasks, such as adjusting lighting and colors, removing imperfections, or even replacing the sky in a landscape photo.

- Object Recognition and Removal: AI can identify and remove objects or people from images, something that previously required manual editing. Tools like TouchRetouch and Adobe Photoshop offer this feature.

- Style Transfer: AI can apply the style of one image to another, creating an artistic effect. This is often used to make photos look like they were painted in the style of famous artists. Tools like Prisma and DeepArt offer this feature.

- Image Enhancement: AI can enhance image quality, improving resolution, reducing noise, and correcting color. Tools like Topaz Gigapixel AI and Let's Enhance offer these features.

- Face Recognition and Editing: AI can identify faces in images and perform edits like smoothing skin, removing blemishes, or even altering facial features. Tools like FaceApp and Photoshop offer these capabilities.

AI-powered video and image editing tools can greatly simplify the editing process, allowing users to create professional-quality visuals with minimal effort. However, these tools also raise ethical and privacy concerns, particularly when used for creating deepfakes or making unauthorized edits to people's faces. Therefore, it's important to use these tools responsibly and ethically.

Personalized content recommendations and curation

Personalized content recommendations and curation have become increasingly important as the volume of content available online continues to grow. Artificial Intelligence (AI) plays a crucial role in personalizing content recommendations and curation by analyzing user data, preferences, and behavior to deliver tailored content suggestions. Here's an overview of how AI is used in personalized content recommendations and curation:

- User Data Analysis: AI algorithms analyze user data, including browsing history, demographic information, and past interactions with content, to identify patterns and preferences. This allows the system to create a profile for each user that helps in suggesting relevant and engaging content.

- Collaborative Filtering: AI can use collaborative filtering techniques to analyze the behavior of similar users and recommend content based on their preferences. For example, if a group of users shares an interest in a specific topic, the system may recommend content related to that topic to other users in the group.

- Content-Based Filtering: AI can also analyze the content itself, identifying features like keywords, topics, categories, or even sentiment. This allows the system to recommend content based on its relevance to the user's interests, rather than relying solely on user behavior.

- Hybrid Approaches: Many AI-driven content recommendation systems use a combination of collaborative filtering and content-based filtering, which can provide more accurate and diverse content suggestions.

- Contextual Recommendations: AI can consider contextual factors, such as time of day, location, or device type, to deliver content recommendations that are relevant to the user's current situation.

- Continuous Learning: AI-driven content recommendation systems are continuously learning and evolving, refining their suggestions as they receive more user data and feedback. This enables them to stay up-to-date with user preferences and trends.

- Examples of AI-driven personalized content recommendations and curation can be found in various platforms and applications:

- Streaming Services: Platforms like Netflix, Spotify, and YouTube use AI algorithms to analyze user behavior and preferences, providing personalized recommendations for movies, shows, music, and videos.

- E-commerce Platforms: Online retailers like Amazon and eBay use AI to analyze user data and provide personalized product recommendations, increasing the likelihood of making a purchase.

- News and Content Aggregators: Apps like Flipboard, Pocket, and Apple News use AI to curate and recommend articles and stories based on user interests and reading habits.

- Social Media Platforms: Social media platforms like Facebook, Instagram, and Twitter use AI algorithms to personalize users' feeds, showing content that is likely to be engaging and relevant.

By delivering personalized content recommendations and curation, AI can enhance the user experience, increase engagement, and provide value to both content consumers and creators. However, it's essential to consider potential privacy concerns and biases that may arise from the collection and analysis of user data, ensuring that these systems are transparent, ethical, and respect user privacy.

AI in social media marketing and management

Artificial Intelligence (AI) has become an indispensable tool for social media marketing and management, helping businesses optimize their strategies, streamline processes, and better engage with their audiences. Here are some ways AI is used in social media marketing and management:

- Content Creation: AI-powered tools can generate human-like text, making it easier to create social media posts, captions, and headlines. Tools like GPT-3, Jarvis, and Kuki.ai can be used for this purpose.

- Content Curation: AI can automate the process of content curation by gathering and organizing relevant content from various sources. Tools like DrumUp, Curata, or ContentStudio can help businesses share valuable content on social media while supplementing their content creation efforts.

- Posting Schedules: AI can analyze engagement data to determine the best times to post content on social media platforms. Tools like Buffer, Hootsuite, or Sprout Social use AI to recommend optimal posting times, maximizing reach and engagement.

- Audience Analysis: AI can analyze large amounts of data to provide insights into audience preferences, demographics, and behavior. This can help businesses create targeted content and ad campaigns. Tools like Audiense or Sprinklr can provide valuable audience insights.

- Sentiment Analysis: AI can analyze social media conversations to identify the sentiment behind user comments and posts. Sentiment analysis can help businesses gauge customer satisfaction, identify trends, and address potential issues. Tools like Brandwatch or Talkwalker offer sentiment analysis features.

- Image Recognition: AI-powered image recognition can identify and analyze visual content, such as logos, products, or scenes in social media posts. This can help businesses track brand mentions, user-generated content, and competitor activity. Tools like GumGum or LogoGrab offer image recognition capabilities.

- Ad Optimization: AI can optimize social media ad campaigns by analyzing data and adjusting targeting, budget allocation, and bidding strategies in real-time. Platforms like Facebook, Instagram, and Twitter have built-in AI algorithms that optimize ad performance.

- Chatbots and Virtual Assistants: AI-powered chatbots and virtual assistants can manage customer inquiries and engage users in real-time conversations on social media platforms. This can enhance customer service and provide valuable insights about user needs and preferences. Tools like ManyChat, Chatfuel, or MobileMonkey can be used to create chatbots for social media platforms.

- Influencer Discovery: AI can analyze social media data to identify influencers who align with a brand's target audience, values, and goals. Tools like Klear, Upfluence, or Heepsy use AI to help businesses find and collaborate with relevant influencers.

AI-driven social media marketing and management tools can save time, improve efficiency, and provide valuable insights that inform content, ad, and engagement strategies. However, it's important to remember that AI is most effective when used in conjunction with human creativity, strategy, and oversight, ensuring that social media efforts remain authentic and aligned with brand values.

AI for Intellectual Property and Licensing

Artificial Intelligence (AI) is transforming the way intellectual property (IP) and licensing are managed and protected. With the increasing volume of IP assets and the growing complexity of global IP regulations, AI-driven solutions can help businesses and individuals effectively navigate the IP landscape. Here are some ways AI is being used in intellectual property and licensing:

- Patent Search and Analysis: AI-powered tools can streamline the patent search process by analyzing large volumes of patent data and identifying relevant patents based on specific criteria. These tools can also help identify potential infringements, find prior art, and uncover licensing opportunities. Examples of AI-driven patent search tools include Ambercite, Derwent Innovation, and PatSnap.

- Trademark Search and Analysis: AI can assist in trademark searches by analyzing existing trademarks in various databases and identifying potential conflicts or similarities. Tools like TrademarkNow and TrademarkVision use AI algorithms to compare trademarks based on visual and textual features, helping users avoid potential infringement issues.

- IP Portfolio Management: AI-driven IP management platforms can help businesses and individuals manage, monitor, and protect their IP assets more efficiently. These tools can automate various IP management tasks, such as docketing, deadline tracking, and document generation. Examples of AI-powered IP portfolio management tools include Anaqua, CPA Global, and Dennemeyer Octimine.

- IP Valuation: AI can analyze large datasets to determine the value of IP assets, taking into account factors such as market trends, licensing potential, and competitive landscape. This can help businesses make informed decisions about IP licensing, acquisition, or divestment. Tools like Patsnap or Cipher offer IP valuation services.

- IP Licensing and Negotiation: AI-driven platforms can streamline the IP licensing process by identifying licensing opportunities, facilitating negotiations, and automating contract generation. Some tools like Loci Nexus, a blockchain-based platform, use AI to match inventors with potential licensees and facilitate the licensing process.

- IP Risk Management: AI can help businesses assess and manage IP risks by monitoring global IP regulations, identifying potential infringement issues, and providing guidance on IP strategy. Tools like Aistemos Cipher or ktMINE can provide IP risk management services.

- IP Litigation Support: AI-powered tools can assist IP litigators by analyzing large volumes of legal documents, identifying relevant case law, and predicting litigation outcomes. Examples of AI-driven legal research tools include ROSS Intelligence, Lex Machina, and Casetext.

AI-driven solutions for intellectual property and licensing can save time, reduce costs, and provide valuable insights that support informed decision-making. However, it's important to remember that AI is most effective when used in conjunction with human expertise and judgment, ensuring that IP strategy and management remain aligned with business goals and legal requirements.

Creating and licensing AI-generated content

Artificial Intelligence (AI) is being increasingly used to generate content in various forms, including text, images, music, and videos. This technology can produce creative works on a scale and at a speed that would be impossible for humans. However, the licensing of AI-generated content raises several legal and ethical questions. Here's an overview of creating and licensing AI-generated content:

Creating AI-Generated Content

AI can generate a wide range of content:

- Text: AI language models, such as GPT-3, can generate human-like text, including articles, stories, poems, scripts, and more.

- Images: AI algorithms, such as DCGANs (Deep Convolutional Generative Adversarial Networks), can create original images, including artworks, photographs, and designs.

- Music: AI can compose original music or mimic the style of existing composers or genres. Tools like AIVA, OpenAI's MuseNet, and Jukin Media are examples of AI that can generate music.

- Videos: AI can create videos, including animations, deepfakes, and even entire films. Tools like Synthesia and DeepArt can create AI-generated videos.

- Licensing AI-Generated Content

- Licensing AI-generated content can be complex because it challenges traditional concepts of authorship and copyright. Currently, copyright law varies significantly by country, but generally, it requires a human author to grant copyright protection. This raises several issues:

- Who is the author? If an AI creates a piece of content, who should be considered the author? Is it the developer of the AI? The user who provided the inputs? Or should the AI itself be considered the author?

- Who owns the copyright? If the AI is considered the author, it cannot own the copyright because, as of now, AI cannot hold legal rights. If the developer or user is considered the author, they might own the copyright, but this depends on the specific laws of each country.

- How to license? If the AI-generated content is considered to be in the public domain (because it has no human author), anyone can use it without obtaining a license. However, if someone owns the copyright, they can license the content to others, usually for a fee.

- As AI-generated content becomes more prevalent, legal systems around the world will need to address these issues. Some possible solutions could include creating new types of copyright for AI-generated content, granting AI the legal status to hold rights, or developing new licensing models specifically for AI-generated content.

In the meantime, companies and individuals who create and use AI-generated content should consult with legal professionals to ensure they are complying with current laws and regulations. This is a rapidly evolving field, and staying informed about legal developments is crucial.

AI-driven patent analysis and valuation

AI-driven patent analysis and valuation are transforming the way businesses and individuals understand and capitalize on intellectual property (IP). By leveraging artificial intelligence (AI), patent holders can gain valuable insights into the value and potential of their patents, allowing them to make more informed decisions about IP strategy and investment. Here's an overview of AI-driven patent analysis and valuation:

AI-Driven Patent Analysis

- AI-powered tools can analyze large volumes of patent data to provide insights on various aspects of patents, such as:

- Patent Landscaping: AI can help create a comprehensive overview of a specific technology or industry sector by analyzing thousands of patents, identifying trends, key players, and emerging technologies.

- Prior Art Search: AI can streamline the process of finding prior art by scanning and comparing patent documents, research papers, and other sources to uncover relevant documents that may challenge the novelty of a patent application.

- Patent Similarity: AI algorithms can assess the similarity between patents by analyzing their textual and structural features, helping users identify potential infringement risks or licensing opportunities.

- Patent Classification: AI can help automate patent classification by assigning patents to specific technology areas or industries based on their content, improving the efficiency of IP management processes.

- Citation Analysis: AI can analyze patent citation networks to identify influential patents, inventors, or organizations, providing insights into the technology landscape and competitive positioning.

- AI-Driven Patent Valuation

- Determining the value of a patent can be challenging, but AI-driven tools can help assess the monetary worth of patents based on factors such as:

- Market Potential: AI can analyze market data, including trends, demand, and competition, to estimate the potential market value of a patented technology.

- Licensing Potential: AI can help determine the potential for licensing a patent by analyzing similar patents, their licensing history, and market demand for the technology.

- Litigation Risk: AI can assess the risk of patent litigation by analyzing the legal landscape, including past lawsuits, infringement risks, and the strength of the patent claims.

- Technological Significance: AI can evaluate the technological significance of a patent by analyzing its novelty, applicability, and potential impact on an industry.

- Patent Portfolio Strength: AI can help businesses evaluate the overall strength of their patent portfolio by analyzing factors such as the number of patents, their quality, and their alignment with the company's strategic goals.

Examples of AI-driven tools for patent analysis and valuation include PatSnap, Anaqua, ktMINE, Cipher, and Derwent Innovation. These tools can provide valuable insights that help businesses and individuals make strategic decisions about patent acquisition, licensing, litigation, and R&D investment.

It is important to remember that AI-driven patent analysis and valuation tools should be used in conjunction with human expertise to ensure that the insights provided are accurate and relevant to the specific context and goals of the patent holder.

AI-based copyright protection and enforcement

AI-based technologies have become increasingly important in copyright protection and enforcement, as they can help automate tasks, analyze large datasets, and provide valuable insights to help safeguard intellectual property (IP). Here's an overview of how AI is used in copyright protection and enforcement:

AI-Based Copyright Protection

- Content Identification: AI-powered algorithms, like machine learning and computer vision, can be used to identify copyrighted content across various formats such as text, images, audio, and video. For instance, YouTube's Content ID system uses AI to compare uploaded content against a database of copyrighted material, allowing copyright owners to take appropriate action.

- Digital Watermarking: AI can enhance digital watermarking techniques, making it harder for unauthorized users to remove or manipulate watermarks. AI-driven watermarking techniques can create adaptive watermarks that are difficult to detect or remove, ensuring that copyrighted content remains protected.

- Plagiarism Detection: AI-powered plagiarism detection tools can analyze and compare large volumes of text to identify instances of potential copyright infringement. Examples of such tools include Turnitin, Copyscape, and Grammarly.

- Image and Video Recognition: AI-driven image and video recognition tools can scan the web for instances of copyrighted images or videos being used without permission. Services like Google's Cloud Vision API, TinEye, and Pixsy can help copyright owners identify unauthorized use of their content.

- Automated Copyright Registration: AI can streamline the process of registering copyrights by automating the collection and organization of data, reducing the time and resources needed to protect IP.

AI-Based Copyright Enforcement

- Infringement Detection: AI algorithms can monitor the internet for instances of copyrighted content being used without permission. By analyzing large amounts of data, AI can identify websites, social media posts, or other online platforms where infringement occurs.

- Takedown Notices: AI-driven tools can automate the process of issuing takedown notices to infringing parties, ensuring that copyrighted content is quickly removed from unauthorized platforms. For instance, tools like DMCA.com and Lumen Database help copyright owners issue takedown requests efficiently.

- Litigation Support: AI-powered tools can assist in copyright litigation by analyzing large volumes of legal documents and case law to support arguments and predict litigation outcomes. Tools like ROSS Intelligence, Lex Machina, and Casetext can provide valuable insights to copyright litigators.

- Settlement and Negotiation: AI can help copyright owners and infringers reach settlements by analyzing historical data and predicting potential outcomes of litigation, providing guidance on the most favorable terms for both parties.

- Copyright Enforcement Networks: AI can be used to create networks of copyright enforcement agents that work together to identify, track, and address copyright infringements. These networks can include AI-driven bots that continuously monitor the web for unauthorized use of copyrighted material.

AI-based copyright protection and enforcement technologies can save time, reduce costs, and improve the effectiveness of IP management. However, it's crucial to remember that AI tools should be used in conjunction with human expertise and judgment to ensure that copyright protection and enforcement strategies remain aligned with legal requirements and business goals.

AI-driven market research and validation

Artificial Intelligence (AI) has become an essential tool for startups and entrepreneurs as they seek to build innovative businesses and disrupt traditional industries. Leveraging AI can provide a competitive advantage, optimize resources, and drive business growth. This section will explore various aspects of AI for startups and entrepreneurship, including idea generation, market analysis, product development, marketing, and customer experience.

Idea Generation

AI can play a crucial role in the ideation phase of startups by uncovering unique business opportunities and innovative ideas. AI-driven tools can analyze large volumes of data, including market trends, consumer behavior, and emerging technologies, to identify potential gaps in the market or opportunities for disruption. By leveraging AI's ability to process and analyze complex information, startups can generate novel ideas and validate their potential before investing time and resources.

Market Analysis

Understanding the market landscape and competition is vital for startups to succeed. AI-driven market analysis tools can provide invaluable insights into the competitive landscape, industry trends, and customer preferences. By analyzing various data sources, including social media, news articles, and financial reports, AI can help entrepreneurs identify growth opportunities, assess market risks, and make informed decisions about product positioning and target audience.

Product Development

AI technologies can streamline the product development process for startups by automating tasks, enhancing decision-making, and improving product quality. For example, AI-driven design tools can help startups create better products by optimizing their features and functionality based on user feedback and market data. AI can also support the development of advanced products and services, such as chatbots, recommendation engines, and predictive analytics solutions, which can differentiate startups from their competitors and drive customer engagement.

Marketing and Advertising

Startups often face limited marketing budgets, making it essential to maximize the impact of their marketing efforts. AI-driven marketing tools can help startups optimize their marketing strategies by providing data-driven insights into customer behavior, preferences, and trends. AI can also support personalized marketing and advertising by tailoring content and messaging to individual users based on their browsing history, demographics, and interests. This level of personalization can lead to higher conversion rates and customer loyalty.

Additionally, AI-powered tools can assist in social media marketing and management by automating content creation, scheduling, and engagement, freeing up time for startups to focus on other aspects of their business.

Customer Experience

- Providing a superior customer experience is crucial for startups to attract and retain customers. AI can support startups in enhancing their customer experience through various means, including:

- Chatbots and virtual assistants: AI-driven chatbots can provide personalized, real-time customer support, answering questions, and resolving issues quickly and efficiently.

- Predictive analytics: AI can analyze customer data to predict their preferences, needs, and future behavior, enabling startups to offer personalized recommendations and proactive support.

- Sentiment analysis: By analyzing customer feedback, reviews, and social media mentions, AI can help startups understand customer sentiment and identify areas for improvement.

- Natural Language Processing (NLP): AI-powered NLP tools can enable startups to understand and analyze unstructured data, such as customer emails, messages, and voice recordings, providing valuable insights into customer behavior and preferences.

Conclusion

AI has become a game-changer for startups and entrepreneurs, offering various opportunities to innovate, optimize resources, and drive business growth. By leveraging AI technologies, startups can generate novel ideas, gain a deep understanding of their market, streamline product development, enhance marketing efforts, and improve customer experience. However, it is important to remember that AI is not a magic solution, and startups must also invest in human expertise, creativity, and judgment to make the most of AI's potential.

As AI technologies continue to evolve and become more accessible, the opportunities for startups and entrepreneurs to harness AI's power will only grow. By embracing AI, startups can differentiate.

Artificial intelligence (AI) has the potential to revolutionize the way businesses conduct market research and validation. As a data-driven technology, AI can help companies gather and analyze large amounts of information, providing valuable insights that enable them to make informed decisions about their products, services, and target markets. In this section, we will explore the various aspects of AI-driven market research and validation, including data collection, analysis, segmentation, and forecasting.

Data Collection

One of the critical components of market research is collecting relevant and reliable data. AI can support this process by automating data collection from various sources such as websites, social media platforms, news articles, and online reviews. AI-powered web scraping tools can extract structured data from unstructured sources, making it easier for businesses to obtain information on their target markets, competitors, and industry trends.

Additionally, AI can help businesses collect data from their customers through chatbots, online surveys, and other interactive tools. By engaging with customers directly, businesses can gather valuable insights into customer preferences, needs, and expectations.

Data Analysis

Once the data has been collected, AI-driven tools can help businesses analyze and process the information to identify patterns, trends, and correlations. Machine learning algorithms, natural language processing (NLP), and sentiment analysis can be used to analyze large volumes of unstructured data, such as text and voice recordings, to gain insights into customer sentiment and behavior.

For example, AI can analyze customer feedback, reviews, and social media mentions to identify common themes, pain points, and preferences. These insights can help businesses better understand their target market and make data-driven decisions about their product offerings, marketing strategies, and customer service initiatives.

Market Segmentation

Market segmentation is the process of dividing a broad target market into smaller, more homogeneous segments based on factors such as demographics, behavior, and needs. AI can support market segmentation by analyzing large datasets to identify patterns and trends that can be used to create distinct customer segments.

For instance, AI-driven clustering algorithms can group customers based on their preferences, purchasing behavior, and other relevant factors. These customer segments can be used to develop targeted marketing campaigns, tailor product offerings, and optimize pricing strategies, ultimately leading to increased customer satisfaction and loyalty.

Competitive Analysis

Understanding the competitive landscape is essential for businesses to succeed. AI-driven market research tools can provide valuable insights into competitors' strategies, strengths, and weaknesses. By analyzing data from various sources, such as websites, financial reports, and social media, AI can help businesses identify their competitors' market positioning, product offerings, and customer engagement strategies.

These insights can enable businesses to make informed decisions about their own strategies, identify potential opportunities for differentiation, and anticipate potential threats from competitors.

Market Validation

Market validation is the process of determining whether a product or service has a viable market demand. AI can support market validation by analyzing customer data, market trends, and competitor information to assess the potential demand for a product or service. For example, AI-driven tools can help businesses identify gaps in the market, understand customer pain points, and predict the likely success of a new product or service.

Additionally, AI can help businesses validate their market assumptions by conducting experiments and analyzing the results. For example, AI-powered

A/B testing tools can help businesses compare the performance of different marketing campaigns, product features, or pricing strategies, providing data-driven insights that can inform future decision-making.

Forecasting

Forecasting is a crucial aspect of market research, as it helps businesses anticipate future trends, demand, and market conditions. AI-driven forecasting tools can analyze historical data and identify patterns that can be used to predict future outcomes. Machine learning algorithms, time series analysis, and other advanced statistical techniques can be used to develop accurate and reliable forecasts.

For instance, AI-powered demand forecasting tools can help businesses predict future sales, allowing them to optimize inventory management, pricing strategies, and marketing efforts. Similarly, AI-driven tools can forecast market trends, enabling businesses to stay ahead of the curve and adapt their strategies accordingly.

Sentiment Analysis

Sentiment analysis is the process of determining the sentiment or emotion expressed in a piece of text, such as customer reviews, social media posts, or news articles. AI-powered sentiment analysis tools can help businesses understand how their customers feel about their products, services, and brand. By analyzing customer feedback and social media mentions, businesses can identify areas for improvement, address customer concerns, and monitor the overall perception of their brand.

Natural language processing (NLP) and machine learning algorithms are used to identify the sentiment expressed in the text, whether it be positive, negative, or neutral. This information can be invaluable in guiding businesses' decision-making processes, such as product development, marketing strategies, and customer service initiatives.

Social Media Analysis

Social media platforms provide a wealth of information about customer preferences, opinions, and behavior. AI-driven tools can help businesses analyze social media data to gain insights into their target market and the effectiveness of their marketing efforts. For example, AI-powered social media monitoring tools can track mentions of a brand, product, or keyword, providing businesses with real-time feedback on customer sentiment and engagement.

Additionally, AI can be used to analyze the performance of social media campaigns by measuring metrics such as engagement, reach, and conversions. This data can be used to optimize social media strategies, target the right audience, and create content that resonates with customers.

Personalization

AI-driven market research tools can help businesses develop a deeper understanding of their customers, enabling them to deliver personalized experiences, products, and services. By analyzing customer data, AI can identify individual preferences, behavior patterns, and needs, allowing businesses to tailor their offerings to each customer segment.

For example, AI-powered recommendation engines can suggest products or content based on a customer's browsing history, purchase behavior, and demographic information. Personalized marketing campaigns can be developed using AI-driven segmentation tools, ensuring that customers receive relevant and engaging content that resonates with their interests and needs.

Conclusion

AI-driven market research and validation offer numerous benefits for businesses, including improved data collection and analysis, enhanced market segmentation, competitive analysis, market validation, forecasting, sentiment analysis, social media analysis, and personalization. By leveraging AI technologies, businesses can gain valuable insights into their target markets, make data-driven decisions, and optimize their products, services, and marketing efforts.

As AI continues to evolve and become more accessible, businesses of all sizes and industries can take advantage of these powerful tools to drive growth, increase customer satisfaction, and stay ahead of the competition. By integrating AI-driven market research and validation into their decision-making processes, businesses can ensure that their strategies are grounded in data and optimized for success.

Building and scaling AI-powered startups

Building and scaling AI-powered startups can be a challenging yet rewarding endeavor. With the rapid advancements in artificial intelligence (AI) technologies, many entrepreneurs are looking to leverage AI to create innovative products, services, and business models that can disrupt traditional industries. In this section, we will discuss the key steps and considerations for building and scaling AI-powered startups, from ideation and team building to product development and market expansion.

Ideation

The first step in building an AI-powered startup is to identify a unique and viable business idea that leverages AI technology to address a specific problem or opportunity. Entrepreneurs should conduct thorough market research to understand the competitive landscape, target customer needs, and potential market gaps. It is crucial to ensure that the AI-driven solution provides significant value and differentiation compared to existing solutions in the market.

Team Building

Building a strong team with diverse skill sets is essential for the success of any startup, particularly those focused on AI. An ideal team should include experts in AI and machine learning, as well as professionals with domain-specific knowledge, product development, marketing, and business development expertise. It is important to create a collaborative culture that encourages innovation, knowledge sharing, and continuous learning.

Product Development

Developing an AI-powered product or service requires a deep understanding of the underlying AI technology and its potential applications. Entrepreneurs should start by defining the product's core features and functionality, and then explore how AI can enhance these aspects to deliver a superior user experience.

During the development process, it is crucial to prioritize data collection and management, as AI models rely heavily on high-quality data for training and optimization. Entrepreneurs should also ensure that their AI-driven solutions are user-friendly, scalable, and easily adaptable to changing market needs and technological advancements.

Validation and Testing

Before launching an AI-powered product or service, it is essential to validate its market fit and technical performance through extensive testing. Startups should conduct alpha and beta tests, gather feedback from early users, and iteratively improve their offerings based on the insights gained. It is also important to consider ethical implications, data privacy, and security when developing AI-driven solutions.

Market Launch

Once the AI-powered product or service has been thoroughly tested and refined, it is time to launch it in the market. Entrepreneurs should develop a go-to-market strategy that includes targeted marketing and sales efforts, strategic partnerships, and customer acquisition channels. To gain traction and credibility, startups should focus on delivering exceptional customer experiences and demonstrating the value of their AI-driven solutions.

Scaling the Business

After successfully launching the AI-powered product or service, the next step is to scale the business. This involves expanding the customer base, entering new markets, and diversifying the product portfolio. To achieve this, startups should:

Continuously refine their product or service based on customer feedback and market trends.

Develop strategic partnerships with other businesses and organizations to expand their reach and customer base.

Consider international expansion and localization of their product or service to cater to global markets.

Leverage AI to optimize and automate various aspects of their operations, such as marketing, customer service, and supply chain management.

Raise additional funding to fuel growth and expansion, either through venture capital, angel investment, or other financing options.

Building and scaling an AI-powered startup can be a complex and challenging process, but it also offers significant opportunities for innovation, growth, and success. By following the steps outlined above and focusing on developing a strong team, a differentiated product or service, and a scalable business model, entrepreneurs can create AI-powered startups that can disrupt industries and deliver significant value to customers and stakeholders. As the AI landscape continues to evolve, the potential for AI-driven startups to transform the way we live and work will only continue to grow.

Securing funding and investments for AI-focused ventures

Securing funding and investments is a critical aspect of launching and scaling AI-focused ventures. With the rapid advancements in AI technology and its potential to disrupt various industries, investors are increasingly interested in backing innovative AI startups. In this section, we will discuss strategies and considerations for securing funding and investments for AI-focused ventures, from preparing your pitch to identifying the right investors and funding sources.

1. Develop a compelling pitch

A strong pitch is essential for attracting investors to your AI-focused venture. Your pitch should clearly articulate the problem you are addressing, your AI-driven solution, the market opportunity, and your competitive advantage. Additionally, it should demonstrate a deep understanding of the underlying AI technology and its potential applications.

To make your pitch more compelling, consider incorporating the following elements:

A clear and concise problem statement that highlights the market need and the limitations of existing solutions.

A demonstration of how your AI-driven solution addresses the problem more effectively and efficiently than alternatives.

Market size and growth projections to showcase the potential for revenue and profitability.

A robust business model that outlines your monetization strategy, target customer segments, and customer acquisition channels.

Evidence of traction, such as customer testimonials, case studies, or key performance metrics.

A roadmap for product development, market expansion, and scaling.

2. Prepare a solid business plan

A comprehensive business plan is a crucial tool for securing funding and investments. Your business plan should provide detailed information on your AI-focused venture, including market research, competitive analysis, financial projections, and a go-to-market strategy. Ensure that your business plan is well-structured, data-driven, and easy to understand, as it will serve as a reference document for potential investors.

3. Assemble a strong team

Investors often consider the strength of the founding team as a key factor in their investment decisions. Assemble a team with diverse expertise, including AI and machine learning, domain-specific knowledge, product development, marketing, and business development. A strong team with a proven track record can instill confidence in investors and increase the likelihood of securing funding.

4. Identify the right investors and funding sources

There are various sources of funding available for AI-focused ventures, including venture capital firms, angel investors, government grants, and incubator or accelerator programs. Research and identify investors who have experience in your industry or a specific interest in AI technology. Targeting the right investors increases your chances of securing funding and establishing valuable partnerships.

5. Network and build relationships

Networking and building relationships with potential investors, industry experts, and other entrepreneurs can increase your visibility and credibility in the AI ecosystem. Attend industry conferences, networking events, and start-up competitions to meet potential investors and showcase your AI-focused venture. Building relationships with potential investors can lead to valuable mentorship, strategic partnerships, and funding opportunities.

6. Demonstrate traction and progress

Investors are more likely to invest in AI-focused ventures that show signs of traction and progress. Demonstrate your venture's growth and development by sharing key performance metrics, customer testimonials, and case studies. Highlight any significant milestones, such as product launches, partnership agreements, or awards, to showcase your venture's potential and credibility.

7. Be prepared for due diligence

Potential investors will likely conduct due diligence before committing to an investment in your AI-focused venture. Be prepared to provide detailed information on your technology, intellectual property, team, financials, and legal matters. Ensure that your documentation is organized and up-to-date, as thorough preparation can expedite the due diligence process and increase your chances of securing funding.

Conclusion

Securing funding and investments for AI-focused ventures requires a combination of a compelling pitch, a solid business plan, a strong team, targeted investor outreach, networking, demonstrated traction, and preparedness for due diligence. By following these strategies

CONCLUSION

As we reach the end of this eBook, it is essential to acknowledge the tremendous potential that AI holds for transforming the financial landscape and enabling individuals and businesses to achieve financial freedom. Embracing the AI revolution and harnessing its power can significantly impact one's financial growth, providing opportunities to create wealth and generate sustainable income streams. In this extended conclusion, we will reiterate the key aspects of AI-driven financial growth, discuss the future prospects and potential advancements in AI, and emphasize the importance of taking action and implementing the strategies for financial freedom.

Embracing the AI revolution for financial growth

Throughout this eBook, we have explored a multitude of strategies and tools that leverage AI technology to help individuals and businesses optimize their financial decision-making, streamline operations, and unlock new revenue streams. By embracing the AI revolution and integrating AI-driven solutions into their financial planning, investment, and business strategies, individuals and organizations can stay ahead of the curve, capitalize on emerging opportunities, and maximize their financial growth.

Some key areas where AI can be leveraged for financial growth include:

Personal finance management: AI-driven tools can help individuals create budgets, track expenses, set savings goals, and provide personalized financial advice based on their unique circumstances. These tools can also facilitate better investment decisions by offering AI-powered investment platforms, robo-advisors for portfolio management, and automated savings and budgeting tools.

Stock market: AI technology can provide valuable insights into the stock market, enabling algorithmic trading and high-frequency trading, as well as AI-powered stock analysis and prediction. These advanced tools can help investors make more informed decisions and optimize their investment strategies.

Real estate: AI can revolutionize the real estate industry by offering smart property management solutions, AI-driven real estate investment analysis, and AI-powered marketing platforms. These tools can help property investors and managers make data-driven decisions and maximize the returns on their investments.

E-commerce: AI can enhance e-commerce businesses by providing AI-powered product recommendation engines, personalized marketing and advertising, and AI-driven pricing and inventory management. These advanced solutions can help e-commerce businesses better understand their customers, optimize their operations, and boost their bottom line.

Content creation: AI technology can streamline content creation processes by offering AI-powered content generation tools, AI-driven video and image editing, and personalized content recommendations and curation. These tools can help businesses create more engaging and relevant content, improving their marketing efforts and customer engagement.

Intellectual property and licensing: AI can play a crucial role in managing intellectual property by providing AI-driven patent analysis and valuation, AI-based copyright protection and enforcement, and creating and licensing AI-generated content. These tools can help businesses protect their intellectual property and monetize their AI-driven innovations.

Startups and entrepreneurship: Entrepreneurs can leverage AI technology to develop and scale AI-powered businesses, conduct AI-driven market research and validation, and build and monetize AI models. AI consulting and strategy development can also help businesses identify market needs and offer AI solutions that cater to those needs.

Future prospects and potential advancements in AI

As AI technology continues to advance and evolve, its potential applications in the financial realm are expected to expand and become even more sophisticated. Developments in areas such as natural language processing, computer vision, and deep learning will enable the creation of more powerful and versatile AI-driven tools, capable of addressing increasingly complex financial challenges and providing even greater value to users Some potential advancements in AI that could impact the financial landscape include:

Improved data analysis and predictive capabilities: With the continuous development of AI algorithms, we can expect even more accurate financial forecasts and personalized financial advice. These advancements will enable investors and businesses to make more informed decisions and better manage their financial risks.

Enhanced automation: As AI technology becomes more sophisticated, we can expect greater levels of automation in various financial domains. This will help businesses streamline their operations, reduce costs, and improve efficiency, ultimately leading to increased profitability.

Greater integration of AI-driven solutions in traditional financial institutions and systems: As AI technology becomes more widely adopted, traditional financial institutions and systems are likely to integrate AI-driven solutions to offer more efficient and accessible financial services. This could lead to a transformation in the way banking, insurance, and other financial services are provided.

Increased democratization of AI technology: The widespread availability of advanced AI-driven tools and platforms is expected to make AI technology more affordable and accessible to individuals and small businesses. This democratization of AI will enable more people to harness the power of AI to improve their financial well-being.

Ethical AI development and the establishment of industry standards and best practices: As the adoption of AI technology continues to grow, there will be a greater emphasis on developing ethical AI solutions and establishing industry standards and best practices. This will help ensure the responsible and transparent use of AI in financial decision-making and foster trust among users.

Taking action and implementing the strategies for financial freedom

The path to financial freedom requires a proactive and strategic approach, and the key to success lies in taking action and implementing the AI-driven strategies discussed throughout this eBook. By leveraging AI technology and harnessing its power in various financial domains, individuals and businesses can make informed decisions, optimize their resources, and accelerate their journey towards financial independence.

To effectively implement these AI-driven strategies, individuals and businesses should:

Develop a deep understanding of AI technology and its potential applications in their respective financial domains. This will enable them to identify AI-driven tools and solutions that align with their financial goals, needs, and preferences.

Integrate AI-driven solutions into their financial planning, investment, and business strategies, while continuously monitoring their performance and adjusting as needed. This will help them stay agile and responsive to the evolving financial landscape and capitalize on emerging opportunities.

Stay informed about the latest advancements in AI technology and explore new AI-driven opportunities as they emerge. By staying up-to-date with the latest developments, individuals and businesses can ensure that they are always at the forefront of the AI revolution and well-positioned to take advantage of new technologies and applications.

Adopt a mindset of continuous learning and adaptation, ensuring they remain agile and responsive to the evolving financial landscape. As AI technology continues to advance, it will be crucial for individuals and businesses to stay ahead of the curve by constantly updating their knowledge, skills, and strategies.

Collaborate with experts and professionals in the AI and financial industries to gain valuable insights and advice on implementing AI-driven strategies. This can help individuals and businesses navigate the complex landscape of AI technology and ensure they are making the most of the available tools and solutions.

In conclusion, the AI revolution presents a wealth of opportunities for individuals and businesses to unlock financial freedom and achieve sustained financial growth. By embracing AI technology, understanding its potential, and taking action to implement AI-driven strategies, individuals and businesses can harness the power of AI to transform their financial future and prosper in the rapidly evolving financial landscape. By remaining proactive and adaptive, one can thrive in this exciting new era of artificial intelligence and secure their financial well-being for years to come.

For the impact of AI on the global economy and businesses, you can refer to the following sources:

- McKinsey Global Institute (2017). Artificial Intelligence: The Next Digital Frontier? [PDF file]. Retrieved from https://www.mckinsey.com/~/media/McKinsey/Industries/Advanced%20Electronics/Our%20Insights/How%20artificial%20intelligence%20can%20deliver%20real%20value%20to%20companies/MGI-Artificial-Intelligence-Discussion-paper.ashx

- PwC (2017). Sizing the prize: What's the real value of AI for your business and how can you capitalise? Retrieved from https://www.pwc.com/gx/en/issues/data-and-analytics/publications/artificial-intelligence-study.html

For AI-driven investment platforms and robo-advisors, you can refer to:

- Statista (2021). Robo-Advisors - worldwide | Statista Market Forecast. Retrieved from https://www.statista.com/outlook/dmo/fintech/robo-advisors/worldwide

- Schwab, C. (2019). The impact of robo-advisors on the future of investment management. Journal of Investing, 28(3), 9-16.

For AI in e-commerce and AI-powered product recommendation engines:

- Retail Dive (2020). 75% of consumers want more human interaction in the future, study finds. Retrieved from https://www.retaildive.com/news/75-of-consumers-want-more-human-interaction-in-the-future-study-finds/558438/

- Accenture (2016). Personalization Pulse Check [PDF file]. Retrieved from https://www.accenture.com/_acnmedia/PDF-2/Accenture-Pulse-Check-Digital-Personalization.pdf

- For AI in the stock market and algorithmic trading:

- Chaboud, A. P., Chiquoine, B., Hjalmarsson, E., & Vega, C. (2014). Rise of the machines: Algorithmic trading in the foreign exchange market. The Journal of Finance, 69(5), 2045-2084.

- Gomber, P., Kauffman, R. J., Parker, C., & Weber, B. W. (2018). On the ubiquitous adoption of algorithmic trading in the capital markets industry. Electronic Markets, 28(4), 429-440.

For AI in real estate and smart property management:

- PwC (2019). Real estate's new frontier: How technology is changing the property sector. Retrieved from https://www.pwc.co.uk/industries/real-estate/insights/real-estates-new-frontier.html

- KPMG (2018). Proptech 3.0: The Future of Real Estate? Retrieved from https://home.kpmg/xx/en/home/insights/2018/07/proptech-3-0-the-future-of-real-estate.html

For AI in content creation and AI-powered content generation tools:

- Zmigrod, R., Mather, G., & Wang, W. Y. (2021). The Language Interpretability Tool: Extensible, Interactive Visualizations and Analysis for NLP Models. In Proceedings of the 2021 Conference of the North American Chapter of the Association for Computational Linguistics: Human Language Technologies: Demonstrations, 40-46.

- Gatt, A., & Krahmer, E. (2018). Survey of the state of the art in natural language generation: Core tasks, applications, and evaluation. Journal of Artificial Intelligence Research, 61, 65-170.

For AI as a Service (AIaaS) and AI-driven software and tools for businesses:

- Deloitte (2017). Artificial intelligence: From expert-only to everywhere. Retrieved from https://www2.deloitte.com/us/en/insights/focus/signals-for-strategists/artificial-intelligence-from-expert-only-to-everywhere.html

- IDC (2019). Worldwide Artificial Intelligence Software Platforms Market Shares, 2018: Steady Growth. Retrieved from https://www.idc.com/getdoc.jsp?containerId=US45340619

For AI in Intellectual Property and Licensing:

- WIPO (2020). WIPO Technology Trends 2019: Artificial Intelligence. Retrieved from https://www.wipo.int/publications/en/details.jsp?id=4386

- U.S. Patent and Trademark Office (2020). Public Views on Artificial Intelligence and Intellectual Property Policy. Retrieved from https://

www.uspto.gov/sites/default/files/documents/USPTO_AI-Report_2020.pdf

For AI in Startups and Entrepreneurship:

- Bughin, J., Hazan, E., Ramaswamy, S., Chui, M., Allas, T., Dahlström, P., ... & Trench, M. (2017). Artificial intelligence: The next digital frontier?. McKinsey Global Institute.

- KPMG (2017). The Changing Landscape of Disruptive Technologies. Retrieved from https://assets.kpmg.com/content/dam/kpmg/xx/pdf/2017/10/the-changing-landscape-of-disruptive-technologies.pdf

Copyright Page

Copyright © [2023] [Kyle Rae)

We hope you find this eBook informative and helpful in your understanding of how blockchain technology can improve government infrastructure.

Thank you for reading.